Student Workbook
Marketing Dynamics
Third Edition

Instructor's Annotated Workbook

Cynthia Gendall Basteri, EdD
Grants Coordinator
Marketing Coordinator Emeritus
Tewksbury Public Schools
Tewksbury, Massachusetts

Brenda Clark, EdD
CTE Director
Jenison High School
Jenison, Michigan

The Goodheart-Willcox Company, Inc.
Tinley Park, Illinois
www.g-w.com

Introduction

This *Student Workbook* is designed for use with the *Marketing Dynamics* textbook. As you complete the activities in this workbook, you will review the facts and concepts presented in the text. The overall objective of these activates is to help you make a smooth transition from your classroom to a meaningful job in the workplace.

The activities in this workbook are divided into chapters corresponding to the chapters in the text. By reading the text first, you have the information needed to complete the activities. Try to complete each activity without referring to the text. Then, check the text for answers to the questions you could not complete. Compare your answers with the information in the text.

The activities will help you gain the skills you need to succeed in the workplace. Some activities, such as true/false questions and math exercises, have "right" answers. Other activities ask you to evaluate various situations, make comparisons, or draw your own conclusions. These activities have neither "right" or "wrong" answers, as they are designed to stimulate creative thinking and help you develop ideas. Do your best to give thoughtful considerations to all your responses.

Copyright © 2014
by
The Goodheart-Willcox Company, Inc.

Previous editions copyright 2006, 2010

All rights reserved. No part of this work may be reproduced, stored, or transmitted in any form or by any electronic or mechanical means, including information storage and retrieval systems, without the prior written permission of
The Goodheart-Willcox Company, Inc.

Manufactured in the United States of America.

ISBN 978-1-61960-348-6
1 2 3 4 5 6 7 8 9 – 14 – 19 18 17 16 15 14 13

Instructor's Annotated Workbook
ISBN 978-1-61960-349-3
1 2 3 4 5 6 7 8 9 – 14 – 19 18 17 16 15 14 13

Contents

Unit 1: Marketing Dynamics
Chapter 1: Marketing and You 5
Chapter 2: Marketing Basics 13
Chapter 3: Business Basics 23
Chapter 4: Marketing Plan 29
Chapter 5: Ethics and Social Responsibility 37

Unit 2: Dynamics of the Economy
Chapter 6: Economic Principles and Systems 45
Chapter 7: Market Forces and Economic Indicators 55
Chapter 8: Business Cycles and the Role of Government 63
Chapter 9: Global Trade 71

Unit 3: Marketplace Dynamics
Chapter 10: Marketing Research 79
Chapter 11: Competition 89
Chapter 12: Targeting a Market 97
Chapter 13: Business-to-Consumer (B2C) Marketing 103
Chapter 14: Business-to-Business (B2B) Marketing 115

Unit 4: Product Dynamics
Chapter 15: Products and Services 123
Chapter 16: New Product Development 133
Chapter 17: Branding 139

Unit 5: Price Dynamics
Chapter 18: Price 149
Chapter 19: Price Strategies 157

Unit 6: Place Dynamics
Chapter 20: Place 167
Chapter 21: Purchasing and Inventory Control 175

Unit 7 Promotion Dynamics

Chapter 22: Communication Process 183
Chapter 23: Promotions 193
Chapter 24: Advertising 203
Chapter 25: Visual Merchandising 211
Chapter 26: Personal Selling 217

Unit 8: Dynamics of Marketing Management

Chapter 27: Management Skills 225
Chapter 28: Marketing Management 233

Unit 9: Professional Development Dynamics

Chapter 29: Planning for Success 245
Chapter 30: Preparing for Your Career 255

Unit 10: Dynamics of Entrepreneurship

Chapter 31: Entrepreneurship 265
Chapter 32: Risk Management 273
Chapter 33: Business Funding 281

Name _____ Date _____ Period _____

CHAPTER 1
Marketing and You

Part 1: Check Your Knowledge

Matching
Write the correct term for each definition on the line provided.

Key Terms

business
career
career clusters
career pathways
consumer
function
functions of business
goal
goal setting
job
long-term goal
market
marketing
marketing professional
need
profession
short-term goal
SMART goals
want

1. Career areas included in the career clusters that consist of ranging from entry-level to those requiring advanced college degrees and years of experience.
   career pathways

2. A goal that can be achieved in less than one year.
   short-term goal

3. A goal that will take a longer time to achieve, usually longer than one year.
   long-term goal

4. Something necessary for survival, such as food, clothing, and shelter.
   need

5. A person who buys products or services and also uses them.
   consumer

Copyright Goodheart-Willcox Co., Inc. 5

6. A general word for a category of activities.
   function

7. The term for all of the activities involved in developing and exchanging products and services.
   business

8. Goals that are specific, measurable, attainable, realistic, and timely.
   SMART goals

9. Something that a person desires, but could live without, such as a new cell phone or a vacation.
   want

10. Production, finance, marketing, and management.
    functions of business

11. The person who helps determine the marketing needs of a company, develops and implements marketing plans, and focuses on customer satisfaction.
    marketing professional

12. Sixteen groups of occupational and career specialties that share common knowledge and skills.
    career clusters

13. Anywhere a buyer and a seller convene to buy and sell goods.
    market

14. Something a person wants to achieve in a specified time period.
    goal

15. Dynamic activities that identify, anticipate, and satisfy customer demand while making a profit.
    marketing

True or False

Decide whether each statement is true or false and enter *T* or *F* on the line provided. If the statement is false, rewrite the statement to make it true.

1. A series of related jobs in the same profession is called a pathway. False. A series of related jobs in the same profession is called a career.

2. A job is the work a person does regularly in order to earn money. True

3. Goal setting is the process of deciding what a person wants to achieve. True

4. The term used for jobs in a business field requiring similar education, training, or skills is career cluster. False. The term used for jobs in a business field requiring similar education, training, or skills is profession.

Chapter 1 Marketing and You

Name _____

5. A need is something that a person desires, but could live without, such as a new cell phone or a vacation. False. A want is something that a person desires, but could live without, such as a new cell phone or a vacation.

Open Response

Write your response to each of the following statements or questions in the space provided. Use complete sentences.

1. What is the difference between a need and a want? Name a business that primarily markets to customer needs and a business that primarily markets to customer wants. Justify your answers.
A need is something necessary for survival, such as food, clothing, and shelter. A need can also be defined as something necessary to function in society. A want is something that a person desires, but could live without, such as a new cell phone or a vacation. Student answers will vary as to the types of businesses that cater to their customers' needs and wants.

2. Name the five levels of careers and describe how one level can lead to the next.
An entry-level position is usually a person's first or beginning job. A career-level position requires employees to have the skills and knowledge for continued employment and advancement in a field. A specialist-level position requires specialized knowledge and skills in a specific field of study but does not supervise other employees. A supervisory-level position requires specialized knowledge and skills and has management responsibility over other employees. An executive level is the highest level position responsible for the planning, organizing and management of a company.

3. Describe the SMART goal process.
The SMART goals process defines goals in ways that are specific, measurable, attainable, realistic, and timely.

4. Describe the role of a marketing professional in a company.
A marketing professional determines the marketing needs of a company, develops and implements marketing plans, and focuses on customer satisfaction.

5. What do all of the careers within any given pathway in a career cluster have in common?
All of the careers within any given pathway in a career cluster share a foundation of common knowledge and skills.

Part 2: Marketing by the Numbers

In 2010, the United States Bureau of Labor and Statistics published the 2010 median pay for a variety of business and financial occupations. The following is a list of those occupations along with the 2010 median pay for each occupation. Review the list carefully. You will use the information in this chart to help you complete the bar graph on the next page.

Occupation	2010 Median Pay
Accountants and Auditors	$61,690
Appraisers and Assessors	$48,500
Budget Analysts	$68,200
Claims Adjusters	$58,460
Cost Estimators	$57,860
Financial Analysts	$74,350
Financial Examiners	$74,940
Human Resource Specialists	$52,690
Insurance Underwriters	$59,290
Loan Officers	$56,490
Logisticians	$70,800
Management Analysts	$78,160
Market Research Analysts	$60,570
Meeting and Event Planners	$45,260
Personal Financial Advisors	$64,750
Purchasing Managers	$58,360
Tax Examiners and Collectors	$49,360

Chapter 1   Marketing and You

Name _____

Use the previous chart and the list of occupations below to create a bar graph in the space that follows. Draw a bar within the graph to indicate the median pay for each occupation. After you create the graph, answer the activity questions. The first one has been done for you.

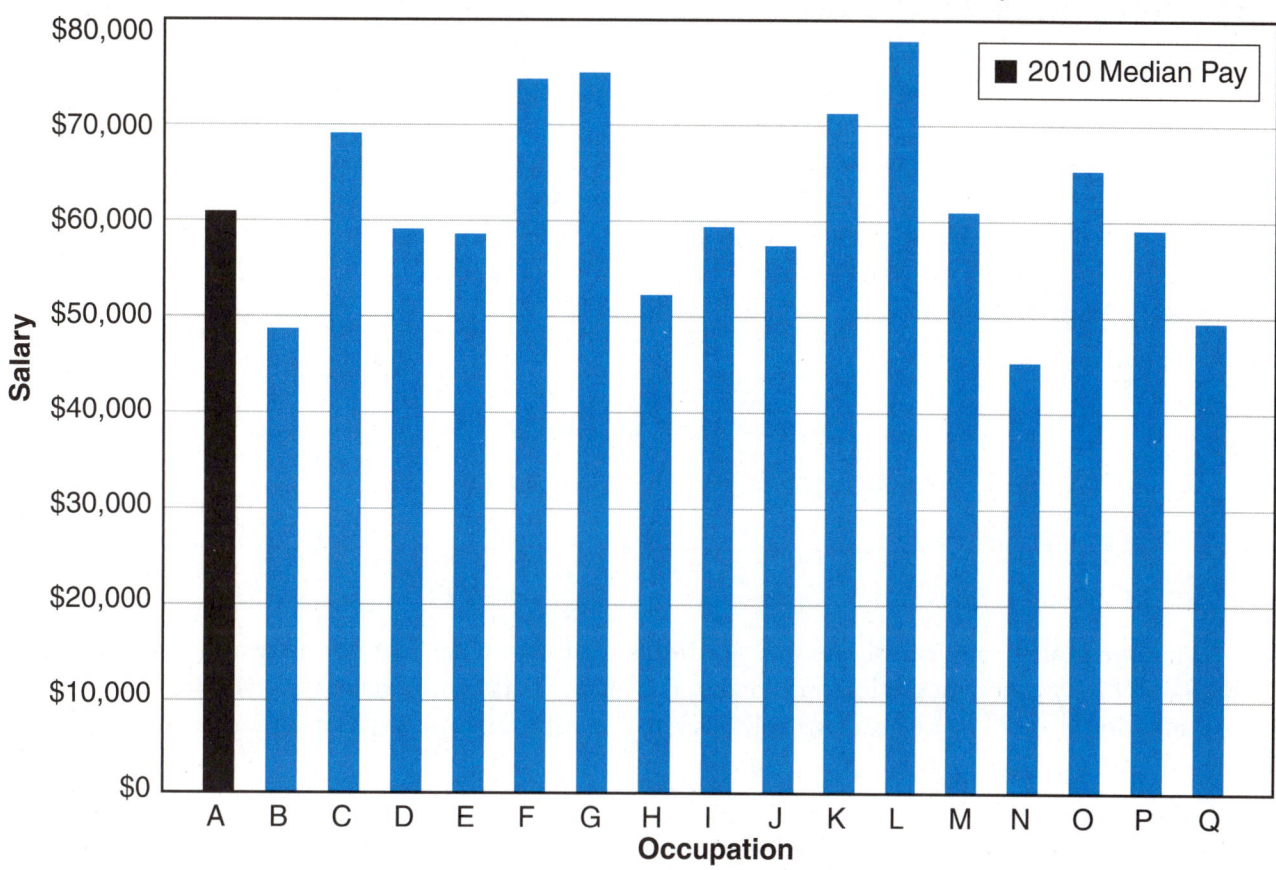

A. Accountants and Auditors
B. Appraisers and Assessors
C. Budget Analysts
D. Claims Adjusters
E. Cost Estimators
F. Financial Analysts
G. Financial Examiners
H. Human Resource Specialists
I. Insurance Underwriters
J. Loan Officers
K. Logisticians
L. Management Analysts
M. Market Research Analysts
N. Meeting and Event Planners
O. Personal Financial Advisors
P. Purchasing Managers
Q. Tax Examiners and Collectors

1. Which occupation had the highest median pay?
   Management Analysts

2. Which occupation had the lowest median pay?
   Meeting, Convention, and Event Planners

3. What is the difference between the highest and lowest salary?
   $32,900

4. Why do you think there is such a large difference in salaries?
   Student answers will vary.

5. Look at the data and then look at the graph. Which one made it easier to answer the questions? Why?
   Student answers will vary.

Part 3: Demonstrate Your Knowledge

Assessing Yourself

There are many marketing careers that fit different interests, skills, and abilities. The first step in moving forward is to honestly assess your aptitudes and abilities. Answer the following questions.

1. In some situations, your worst fault can become your greatest strength and your greatest strength can become your worst fault. For example, suppose you are often criticized for talking too much in class. You might have a great strength in speaking or getting along with people. For what are you most often criticized? List a weakness or fault, and then explain how it could become a strength.

   Student answers will vary.

2. Explain how one of your strengths could be a benefit at work.

   Student answers will vary.

3. What are your strongest abilities and aptitudes? Think of what you do easily and well. Also, think of why others might look up to you. For example, do your friends ask you for help with their computers? List at least two abilities and/or aptitudes and explain why you chose them.

   Student answers will vary.

4. Many careers are based on specific rules or procedures that must be followed. Examples include accounting, banking, copyediting, law, and medicine. Other careers emphasize creativity and individual approaches. Examples include advertising, sales, and visual merchandising. Both kinds of careers can be exciting, but in different ways. Describe how you feel about following set rules and procedures. Would you be more inclined to enjoy a job based on rules or one that emphasizes individuality? Explain why.

   Student answers will vary.

5. Are you a lark or an owl? In other words, do you wake up, hit the floor running, and feel most energetic in the morning and afternoon? Or, do you wake up slowly and feel more energetic as the day goes on? Larks, or morning people, generally do well with standard business days, which start between 7:30 and 9:00 a.m. and end by 5:00 p.m. Owls, or night people, might consider careers with evening hours or flexible schedules, such as consulting, hospitality, and retail. Are you a lark or an owl? Choose one, then describe your reason for choosing it.

   Student answers will vary.

Chapter 1 Marketing and You

Name _____

Apply Your Knowledge

1. What does it mean to say, "Without customers, there would be no businesses?"
   Student answers will vary.

2. List three of your needs and three of your wants. In general, would you say that you have more needs than wants or more wants than needs? Explain why.
   Student answers will vary.

3. In today's society, why is marketing much more than just promoting a product?
   Student answers will vary.

4. In Chapter 1, you read that there are many foundation skills that are necessary for success in any career. Choose one of the five categories of foundation skills and describe why they are necessary to be successful.
   Student answers will vary.

5. Why can it be said that the opportunities for careers in marketing are endless?
   Student answers will vary.

Part 4: Be Your Own Leader

Developing Your Leadership Skills

Marketing requires leadership skills. What makes a great leader? What is the difference between a good leader and a great leader? Think about the people you feel are great leaders. Think about the qualities those leaders possess.

1. Name two people you think are great leaders. They may be people you know personally, people from history, celebrities, athletes, or others. Explain why you believe they are a great leader.

Leader 1 *Student answers will vary.*

Explanation *Student answers will vary.*

Leader 2 *Student answers will vary.*

Explanation *Student answers will vary.*

2. List the top 10 qualities that you think great leaders posses. Once you have listed those qualities, interview an adult to find out the 10 qualities he or she thinks a great leader possesses. Compare the two lists and write an analysis of the similarities and differences between them.

Your List	Interviewee List
Student answers will vary.	*Student answers will vary.*

3. Review the list of qualities that you wrote in the previous question. Prepare a plan for developing leadership qualities Identify those qualities that you feel that you possess with a plus sign (+) and those qualities that you need to work on with a minus sign (–). For those qualities with a minus sign, write a plan to work on developing those qualities.

Student answers will vary.

Name _____ Date _____ Period _____

CHAPTER 2
Marketing Basics

Part 1: Check Your Knowledge

Matching

Write the correct term for each definition on the line provided.

Key Terms

channel
channel management
customer
customer satisfaction
dynamic
four Ps of marketing
good
idea
marketing concept
marketing-information management (MIM)
marketing mix
market planning

place
price
product
product/service management
profit
promotion
public relations
purchase incentive
selling
service
target market

1. Something that is constantly changing, such as the needs and wants of customers.
   dynamic

2. An individual or group who buys products.
   customer

3. A physical item that can be touched.
   good

4. The degree to which customers are pleased with a company's goods or services.
   customer satisfaction

5. An item that helps persuade a customer to make a purchase, such as rewarding loyal customers with discounts or free products.
   purchase incentive

Copyright Goodheart-Willcox Co., Inc.   13

6. The process of communicating with potential customers in an effort to influence their buying behavior.
   promotion

7. Product, price, place, and promotion.
   four Ps of marketing

8. The amount of money requested or exchanged for a product.
   price

9. A plan of action for marketing a product; it consists of the decisions made about each of the four Ps for that product.
   marketing mix

10. The specific group of customers whose needs a company will focus on satisfying.
    target market

11. A concept, cause, issue, image, or philosophy that can be marketed.
    idea

13. Anything that can be bought or sold.
    product

14. A type of promotion that focuses on creating a positive image of a company rather than the product.
    public relations

15. The money that a business has left after all the expenses and costs of running the business are paid.
    profit

16. Determining which products a business should offer to meet customer needs.
    product service management

17. Involves gathering and analyzing information about markets, customers, industry trends, new technology, and the competing businesses.
    MIM

18. Includes all personal communications with customers.
    selling

19. The different routes products take from the producers to the customers.
    channel

20. The activities involved in getting a product or service to the end users, which is also known as distribution.
    place

21. An action that is done for you, usually for a fee.
    service

Chapter 2 Marketing Basics **15**

Name _____

True or False

Decide whether each statement is true or false and enter *T* or *F* on the line provided. If the statement is false, rewrite the statement to make it true.

1. Market planning involves creating an actionable marketing plan designed to achieve business goals. True

2. Channel management involves handling activities involved in getting products through the different channels. True

3. The marketing concept is an approach to business that focuses on achieving profit goals regardless of customer satisfaction. False. The marketing concept is an approach to business that focuses on satisfying customers as the means of achieving profit goals.

4. The word dynamic describes something that is constantly the same. False. The word dynamic describes something that is constantly changing.

5. Marketing means the same as advertising. False. Marketing means more than advertising and contains the four P's: product, place, price and promotion.

6. The objective of place is to deliver exactly what the end user wants—at the right time, in the right place, and at the right price. True

7. The three elements of the marketing concept are customer satisfaction, total company approach, and promotion. False. The three elements of the marketing concept are customer satisfaction, total company approach, and profit.

8. Marketing-oriented companies believe that every interaction with a customer should be viewed as a marketing opportunity. True

9. The different routes a product takes from the producers to the customers are called channels. True

10. The pricing function does *not* include researching and analyzing competitors' pricing. False. The pricing function does include researching and analyzing competitors' pricing.

Copyright Goodheart-Willcox Co., Inc.

Part 2: Marketing by the Numbers

Graphs

The following table shows a year of sales for a cell phone company. At first glance, all you see is a group of numbers. Putting the information into a line graph provides a more dynamic representation of a sales history.

Cell Phone Sales			
Month	Sales	Month	Sales
January	$289,000	July	$310,000
February	$329,000	August	$352,000
March	$304,000	September	$375,000
April	$307,000	October	$294,000
May	$321,000	November	$449,000
June	$389,000	December	$453,000

Using the information from the chart, create a bar graph in the space that follows. After you create the graph, answer the activity questions.

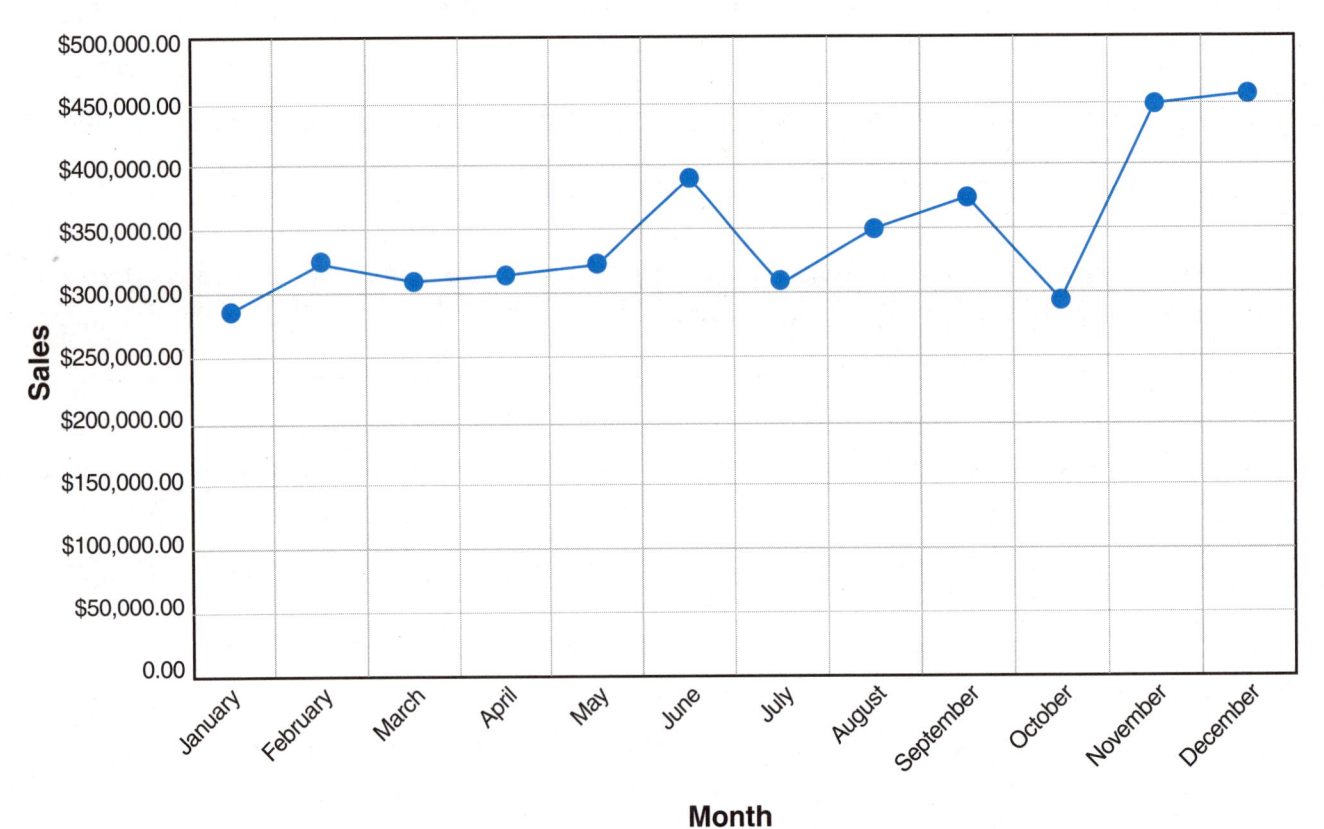

Chapter 2   Marketing Basics

Name _____

Use the information from the previous page to answer the questions below.

1. During which month were the cell phone sales the highest?
   December

2. During which month were the cell phone sales the lowest?
   January

3. What is the difference between the highest monthly sales and the lowest?
   $164,000

4. Why do you think there was such a large difference in sales?
   Student answers will vary.

5. Look at the data and then look at the graph. Which one made it easier to answer the questions? Why?
   Student answers will vary.

Part 3: Demonstrate Your Knowledge

Open Response

Write your response to each of the following statements or questions in the space provided. Use complete sentences.

1. How can a person be considered a product? Give two examples to explain your answer.
   Student answers will vary.

2. Describe several ways to organize marketing activities.
   Student answers will vary.

3. Why is setting the best price important for both business success and customer satisfaction? Give two examples to explain your answer.
   Student answers will vary.

4. How does the marketing concept benefit customers?
   Student answers will vary.

5. Describe the seven functions of marketing. Is there a difference between how the seven functions are handled in a large company versus a small company? Explain your answer.
   Student answers will vary.

Apply Your Knowledge

Changes are always occurring in the world of marketing. A marketing mix that works well for one situation will not always work well for other situations. In each situation, identify what changed in the space provided.

1. Mark has just been offered a deal. For one-half the retail price, he can buy a warehouse full of videos and music on tape cassettes. Mark plans to rent a space at the mall for November and December and sell the cassettes for twice what he paid. Even after paying the rent and advertising, he expects to make a good profit. Do you think Mark will make the profit he expects? Explain your answer. What change has occurred that might affect Mark's plans?
   Student answers will vary.

Chapter 2 Marketing Basics

Name _____

2. Despite the high prices, products such as organic produce; meatless hamburgers and sausage; and low-fat, low-carbohydrate, and low-calorie foods are selling quite well. Why are customers willing to pay more for these products? What has changed?

Student answers will vary.

3. In the 1970s, convertible-top automobiles declined in popularity. Several manufacturers stopped making this style of car. Concerns about safety were a major factor. Recently, convertibles have become popular again. Why are convertibles popular again? What has changed?

Student answers will vary.

4. Golden Circle is a mail-order company that sells safety items to families with young children. Popular items include cabinet door locks and child car seats. Golden Circle has always taken pride in its customer base and rewarded repeat customers. However, sales have been steadily decreasing. Why might sales be decreasing? What may have changed? What should Golden Circle do to increase sales?

Student answers will vary.

5. O'Hanlon's is a children's clothing store located in Buckram. It was once known as *Furniture City* because of the many furniture manufacturers located there. In recent years, all of Buckram's furniture plants have closed due to increased foreign competition. Back-to-school shopping was once the mainstay of O'Hanlon's business, but the last few Augusts have been very slow. Why are sales falling? What may have changed?

Student answers will vary.

Copyright Goodheart-Willcox Co., Inc.

Part 4: Be Your Own Leader

Starting a Conversation

As a marketer, you will deal with many people in person, on the phone, and even electronically through e-mail, social media, and other technologies. Those first introductions can be awkward if you do not know what to say when you first meet someone.

Have a simple introduction prepared that can be used for any purpose, whether you are dealing with a vendor, meeting a classmate for the first time, interviewing for a potential job, or sending an e-mail. A useful introduction that is also easy to remember is GNAP, which stands for greeting, name, affiliation, and purpose.

G = Greeting. Your greeting for marketing purposes should be formal. Use Hello, Good Morning, Good Afternoon, or Good Evening. Avoid using slang, such as Hi or Hey.

N = Name. Use your full name when meeting other marketers or businesspeople, but then tell the person what name you go by. For example, my name is Kristine Heykoop but people call me Kris. If meeting a classmate for the first time, it is appropriate to use a shortened name.

A = Affiliation. Your affiliation is your association with a group, organization, or school. For example, you might be affiliated with Jenison High School, Trenton FBLA, or Apple Computers.

P = Purpose. What is your purpose for the call, e-mail, contact, or social media connection? For example, you might say, "I am here for an interview with Mr. Kamal Patel."

1. For the following scenarios, write how you would GNAP the person in a sentence format. For example, the GNAP for this introduction follows: Hello, my name is Gregory Phillips. I am from Loyola University, and I am here for a ten o'clock interview with Shania Washington.

   G = Hello,

   N = my name is Gregory Phillips.

   A = I am from Loyola University,

   P = and I am here for a ten o'clock interview with Shania Washington.

   A. You are scheduled to interview for a marketing apprenticeship with the New York Nets. The person you will be interviewing with is Moses Abrams. You are currently attending a university and will be graduating in the spring.

   G = Student answers will vary.

   N =

   A =

   P =

   B. As a manager of your school-based enterprise, you need to contact a sales representative from the Otis Spunkmeyer company to place a product order.

   G = Student answers will vary.

   N =

   A =

   P =

Chapter 2 Marketing Basics

21

Name _____

C. As a marketing intern with Hilton Hotels, you have been asked to work with the local chamber of commerce on a tourism campaign. You are to contact Maria Sanchez, the chamber's president.

G = _Student answers will vary._____

N = _____

A = _____

P = _____

2. Practice GNAP with one other classmate. Before you practice, there are some additional things to add to GNAP. When introducing yourself in person, you need to have good eye contact, give a firm handshake, stop walking before you start talking, keep your body relaxed but still, and have an enthusiastic voice. Choose one of the previous scenarios for your practice. Use the evaluation form that follows to evaluate each other.

| | Presenter ||
	YES	NO
EYES	Student answers will vary.	Student answers will vary.
Maintained eye contact without staring?		
HANDS		
Gave a firm handshake?		
Kept hands visible?		
VOICE		
Enthusiastic?		
Good intonation?		
Used slang words?		
Spoke too fast?		
GNAP		
Greeting?		
Name?		
Affiliation?		
Purpose?		

Copyright Goodheart-Willcox Co., Inc.

Name _____ Date _____ Period _____

CHAPTER 3
Business Basics

Part 1: Check Your Knowledge

Matching
Write the correct term for each definition on the line provided.

Key Terms

adding value
barter
business market
business-to-business (B2B)
business-to-consumer (B2C)
commercial
consumer market
contract
corporation
finance
form utility
industry
information utility
liability
management
medium of exchange
money
nonprofit organization
partnership
place utility
possession utility
production
sole proprietorship
store of value
time utility
time value of money
unit of value
utility
wage

1. Money used in exchange for goods and services.
   medium of exchange

2. Legal responsibility.
   liability

3. Consists of customers who buy products for use in a business.
   business market

4. Value added when products are available at convenient places.
   place utility

Copyright Goodheart-Willcox Co., Inc.   23

5. Defined by the US Supreme Court as "an artificial being, invisible, intangible, and existing only in contemplation of the law."

   corporation

6. Refers to buying and selling on a large scale.

   commercial

7. Includes all activities involving money.

   finance

8. A common measure of what something is worth or what something costs.

   unit of value

9. A legally binding agreement.

   contract

10. The exchange of one good or service for another good or service.

    barter

11. The consumer market of businesses selling primarily to individual consumers.

    business-to-consumer (B2C)

13. A group of businesses that produce similar goods or services.

    industry

14. Money earned for working.

    wage

15. Consists of customers who buy products for their own use.

    consumer market

16. Value added when it becomes easier for a customer to acquire a product.

    possession utility

17. The characteristics of a product that satisfies human wants and needs.

    utility

18. An organization that exists to serve some public purpose.

    nonprofit organization

19. The process of controlling and making decisions about a business.

    management

20. Anything of value that is accepted in return for goods or services.

    money

Chapter 3 Business Basics

Name _____

21. Value added when marketing provides information about a product to a customer.
    information utility

22. The business market of businesses selling primarily to other businesses.
    business-to-business (B2B)

23. The idea that money is worth more today than would be in the future.
    time value of money

24. Any activity related to making a product.
    production

25. The relationship between two or more people who join to create a business.
    partnership

26. Value added when products are made available at the times that customers need and want them.
    time utility

27. An item that can be saved, or stored, and used at a later date while holding its value.
    store of value

28. A business owned by one person.
    sole proprietorship

29. Involves enhancing a feature or service that inspires a customer to purchase.
    adding value

30. Value added when a business changes the form of something to make it more useful.
    form utility

Part 2: Marketing by the Numbers

Medium of Exchange

In the United States, the medium of exchange is the US dollar. For most cash transactions, the customer usually does not have the exact change. Even though a computerized cash register tells you how much change the customer gets, it does not tell you the combination of bills and coins.

Imagine you are a cashier. Your cash register has a cash drawer with these types of coins: pennies, nickels, dimes, and quarters. It also has the following bills: $1, $5, $10, and $20.

The following chart lists sales you made in one shift. The first column lists the sales. The second column lists the amount of cash given by the customer for each sale. Calculate the change due the customer and record it in the third column called *Change Due*. In the remaining columns, indicate how you would return that change in the fewest coins and bills. The first sale is completed for you as an example.

Total	Amount Given	Change Due	$20	$10	$5	$1	$0.25	$0.10	$0.05	$0.01
$ 17.99	$ 20.00	$ 2.01				2				1
$ 16.43	$ 20.00	$ 3.57				3	2		1	2
$ 8.24	$ 10.00	$ 1.76				1	3			1
$ 9.72	$ 20.00	$ 10.28		1			1			3
$ 13.63	$ 20.00	$ 6.37			1	1	1	1		2
$ 4.98	$ 10.00	$ 5.02			1					2
$ 2.99	$ 5.00	$ 2.01				2				1
$ 63.58	$ 100.00	$ 36.42	1	1	1	1	1	1	1	2
$ 7.90	$ 20.00	$ 12.10		1		2		1		
$ 32.36	$ 50.00	$ 17.64		1	1	2	2	1		4
$ 11.21	$ 20.21	$ 9.00			1	4				
$ 44.52	$ 60.00	$ 15.48		1	1		1	2		3
$ 63.71	$ 80.00	$ 16.29		1	1	1	1			4
$ 85.34	$ 100.00	$ 14.66		1		4	2	1	1	1
$ 76.83	$ 100.00	$ 23.17	1			3		1	1	2
$ 91.27	$ 100.00	$ 8.73			1	3	2	2		3
$ 126.87	$ 130.00	$ 3.13				3		1		3
$ 153.25	$ 200.00	$ 46.75	2		1	1	3			
$ 191.99	$ 200.00	$ 8.01			1	3				1
$ 156.23	$ 160.00	$ 3.77				3	3			2
$ 189.02	$ 200.02	$ 11.00		1		1				
$ 166.98	$ 200.00	$ 33.02	1	1		3				2
$ 153.92	$ 160.00	$ 6.08			1	1			1	3

Chapter 3   Business Basics

Name _____

Part 3: Demonstrate Your Knowledge

B2B or B2C Situation

Is it a business-to-business (B2B) or business-to-consumer (B2C) situation? Read the following scenarios and write either B2C or B2B in the blanks.

1. Green Sea is a turf farm that grows hundreds of acres of lawn grass. The turf is cut into strips with roots and soil attached, rolled up, and sold to customers who replant the turf to create instant lawns. Green Sea sold 50 acres of turf to Amanda Hicks and Sons Landscaping. Hicks will use the turf for a customer who is building a new golf course.

   B2B

2. Janiss and Antwon Williams are building a new house on a half acre of land. They plan to buy the turf from Green Sea.

   B2C

3. Rosaria owns a gift shop. Twice a year, she travels to Atlanta for the semiannual Gift Show, where hundreds of dealers and manufacturers display their new jewelry, vases, home decorations, and other gifts. Rosaria orders items for her shop.

   B2B

4. Immaculate Interiors is a cleaning service with both residential and commercial customers. The company regularly buys floor wax, mops, and gasoline for its van.

   B2B

5. Immaculate Interiors has just arranged to clean Janiss and Antwon Williams' home on a regular basis.

   B2C

6. Immaculate Interiors has contracts to clean several retail stores, a museum, and an office building.

   B2B

Copyright Goodheart-Willcox Co., Inc.

Part 4: Be Your Own Leader

Leaders Motivate

1. What is motivation? As a leader, it is important to motivate others to follow your lead. Write a paragraph defining your definition of motivation. Provide an example of a time when you were either able to motivate others or someone motivated you.

   Student answers will vary.

2. Once you have written your own definition of motivation and an example, share them with one other student. Use both of your original definitions to write a new definition of motivation.

   Student answers will vary.

3. Do an Internet search to find and read an article about motivating others. The article should be a minimum of one page in length. Write a summary of the article. Your summary should be at least two paragraphs in length using complete sentences. Use at least two direct quotes from the article in your summary. Make sure to use quotation marks to identify when you are quoting the source material. After writing the summary, list your Key Takeaways, or what you learned or felt were most important to remember.

   Title of Article: Student answers will vary.   Author: _____

   Date of Article: _____   Number of pages: _____

   Source: _____

   Summary:
   Student answers will vary.

   Key Takeaways (at least two):
   Student answers will vary.

Name _____ Date _____ Period _____

CHAPTER 4
Marketing Plan

Part 1: Check Your Knowledge

Matching

Write the correct term for each definition on the line provided.

Key Terms

action plan
market segmentation
market share
marketing objective
marketing plan
marketing strategy
marketing tactic
metric
mission statement
place strategy

price strategy
product strategy
promotion strategy
promotional mix
return on investment (ROI)
situation analysis
SWOT analysis
template
unique selling proposition (USP)
vision statement

1. The company message to customers about why the business exists.
   mission statement

2. The process of dividing a large market into smaller groups.
   market segmentation

3. Lists the strengths, weaknesses, opportunities, and threats the business faces.
   SWOT analysis

4. A decision marketers use to help make about what products a business should sell.
   product strategy

5. The percentage of total sales in a market that is held by one business.
   market share

6. A document that already has a basic format that can be used many times.
   template

Copyright Goodheart-Willcox Co., Inc.   29

7. The overall goal for the future of the company.
   vision statement

8. A document describing business and marketing objectives and the strategies and tactics to achieve them.
   marketing plan

9. A combination of the elements used in a promotional campaign.
   promotional mix

10. A decision about which selling, advertising, sales promotions, and public relations activities to pursue in the promotional mix.
    promotion strategy

11. A statement of how your company is different from the competition or how your products are better than the competition.
    unique selling proposition

12. A decision about how and where the products will be produced, acquired, shipped, and sold to customers.
    place strategy

13. A snapshot of the environment in which a business has been operating over a given time, usually the last 12 to 16 months.
    situation analysis

14. Standard of measurement.
    metric

15. A decision made about product, price, place, or promotion.
    marketing strategy

16. A business decision about pricing and how prices are set to make a profit.
    price strategy

17. A ratio that shows the efficiency of an investment by comparing the gains from the investment to its cost.
    return on investment

18. The goal a business wants to achieve during a given time, usually one year, by implementing the marketing plan.
    marketing objective

19. Includes a detailed time line, the budget, and the metrics to evaluate the effectiveness of any campaigns.
    action plan

20. A specific activity to carry out a marketing strategy.
    marketing tactic

Chapter 4   Marketing Plan

Name _____

True or False

Decide whether each statement is true or false and enter T or F on the line provided. If the statement is false, rewrite the statement to make it true.

1. Every marketing plan is unique and will change over time. True

2. Preparing a marketing plan is relatively easy. False. Preparing a marketing plan takes time and research.

3. Part of a price strategy is how your prices compare to the competition. True

4. Place strategies involve decisions only about a physical location. False. Place strategies involve decisions about not only a physical location but how goods or services are distributed.

5. In many companies, the marketing manager may be responsible for all of the promotion strategies. True

6. In a marketing plan, the business overview identifies what makes the company unique and why it is successful. True

7. A business can determine where to go and how to get there even if it does not know where it has been. False. A business cannot determine where to go or how to get there without knowing where it has been.

8. The internal environment is the condition of the local and national economies. False. The external environment is the condition of the local and national economies.

9. Detailed market research is often part of the target market section of a marketing plan. True

10. The Marketing Tactics section of a marketing plan is usually the shortest part. False. Marketing Tactics may be the longest section of the marketing plan because it lists many specific activities.

Copyright Goodheart-Willcox Co., Inc.

Part 2: Marketing by the Numbers

Analyzing Market Share

The bottled water industry is very competitive. The industry market leaders are constantly battling for more market share. Market share is one competitor's percentage of the total sales in a specific market.

The following table shows data for the top 10 bottled water companies in 2012. In the Market Share column, compute the market share percentage using the total dollar sales. Leave the other columns blank.

Rank	Company	Dollar Sales	Market Share (%)	Convert Market Share % to a Decimal (Divide by 100)	Multiply by 360°	Round to the nearest degree (°)
1	Private Label	$1,030,281,682	15.4%	.154	55.44°	55°
2	Aquafina	$689,084,502	10.3%	.103	37.08	37
3	Dasani	$662,323,939	9.9%	.099	35.64	36
4	Glaceau Vitaminwater	$642,253,516	9.6%	.096	34.56	35
5	Poland Spring	$401,408,448	6.0%	.06	21.6	22
6	Nestle Pure Life	$388,028,166	5.8%	.058	20.88	21
7	Glaceau Smartwater	$381,338,025	5.7%	.057	20.52	21
8	Deer Park	$254,225,350	3.8%	.038	13.68	14
9	Glaceau Vitaminwater Zero	$214,084,505	3.2%	.032	11.52	12
10	Ozarka	$200,704,224	3.0%	.03	10.8	11
	Total Top 10 Companies	$4,863,732,357	72.7%	.727	261.72	262
	Total Other Companies in Industry	$1,826,408,437	27.3%	.273	98.28	98
	Industry Total	$6,690,140,794	100%	1.0	360	

Chapter 4   Marketing Plan

Name _____

Visualizing Market Share Using Pie Charts

In this activity, you will create circle graphs. A circle graph is a way of showing the relationship of a part to a whole. A circle graph is like a pie and is sometimes called a *pie chart*.

Circle graphs are used to graph information recorded in percentages. To make an accurate circle graph, you must remember that any circle can be divided into 360° (degrees). Follow these steps for creating a pie chart.

1. Record data as percentages. The percentages should total 100% (or very close to 100%).
2. Change the percentage to the equivalent decimal by dividing the percentage amount by 100. For example, $\frac{15.4\%}{100} = .154$
3. Next, multiply each decimal by 360. For example, .154 x 360 = 55.44. This calculation gives the number of degrees in the circle for each section of the graph.
4. In the last column, round that number either up or down to the nearest whole number (no decimals). For example, 55.44 rounded to the nearest whole number is 55. The total degrees should equal 360° (or very close to 360°).
5. Create a circle graph. Use a protractor to mark off the number of degrees for each section. If one is not available, use your best guess.

Use the chart that shows the top 10 bottled water companies in 2012. Follow the directions directions (numbers two–five) to fill in the remaining three columns of the table. Finally, use the information in your completed table to construct your own pie chart in the space that follows. You may choose to use different colors to create the pie chart. Identify each company and its corresponding color using the Key List provided.

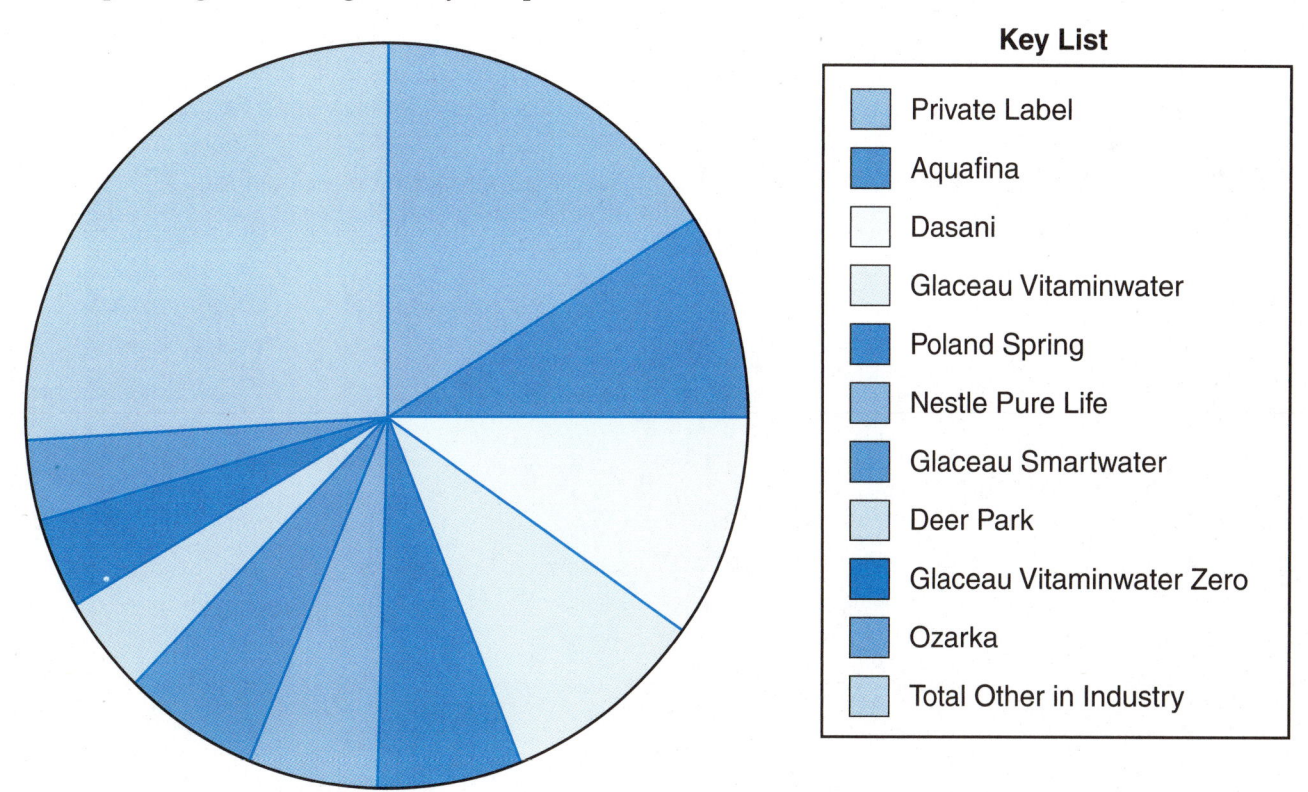

Key List

- Private Label
- Aquafina
- Dasani
- Glaceau Vitaminwater
- Poland Spring
- Nestle Pure Life
- Glaceau Smartwater
- Deer Park
- Glaceau Vitaminwater Zero
- Ozarka
- Total Other in Industry

Copyright Goodheart-Willcox Co., Inc.

Part 3: Demonstrate Your Knowledge

Open Response

Write your response to each of the following statements or questions in the space provided. Use complete sentences.

1. Why is choosing target market an important decision for a marketer?
   Student answers will vary.

2. Choose a product you have seen advertised. Describe the marketing strategy for that product and include the target market and the marketing mix.
   Student answers will vary.

3. Marketing mix decisions are interrelated. Explain what this means.
   Student answers will vary.

4. Conduct a situation analysis for a business that you go to frequently. What factors influence that business' marketing strategy?
   Student answers will vary.

5. How does target marketing allow a small business to compete with larger businesses?
   Student answers will vary.

Chapter 4 Marketing Plan

Name _____

Part 4: Be Your Own Leader

Leaders Motivate

As a leader, you know it is important to motivate others, but what motivates you? Make a list of those things that motivate you. In the second column, make a list of those things that do *not* motivate you, or cause you to *not* want to do something.

1. What motivates me:
Student answers will vary.

2. What does not motivate me:
Student answers will vary.

3. There are two types of motivation—internal and external. People who are motivated externally are motivated by things outside of themselves and/or by how others view them. People who are motivated internally are motivated by things inside themselves and/or how they view themselves. At times, every person is motivated both internally and externally. However, as individuals, people tend to respond better to one than the other. Read the following statements to determine if you respond best to internal or external motivators. Choose the response that best represents you in each situation. There are no right or wrong answers.

A. You have been asked to be a CTSO officer. You decide to run because
Student answers will vary.

___1. it will look great on your college applications.

___2. it will help you to become a better leader.

B. An internship has opened up with a local marketing firm and with a local sports team. You choose the internship that
Student answers will vary.

___1. pays the most.

___2. lets you learn the most.

Copyright Goodheart-Willcox Co., Inc.

C. Two friends invite you to different events at the same time on the same day. Which friend do you choose for the invite?
Student answers will vary.

___1. The friend that is most popular.

___2. The friend that is the most interesting.

D. What would you rather do?
Student answers will vary.

___1. Take a class that will help you improve your GPA.

___2. Take a class that will challenge you without concern about your GPA.

E. What means the most to you?
Student answers will vary.

___1. What others think of you.

___2. What you think of you.

F. You have been asked to watch a younger relative. You will do it
Student answers will vary.

___1. if you get paid.

___2. to help out a relative.

Add up the total number of 1s you checked and write the answer here. _____

Add up the total number of 2s you checked and write the answer here. _____

If you checked more 1s, then you are more externally motivated. If you checked more 2s, then you are more internally motivated. Now, review the list you made earlier about what motivates you and what does *not* motivate you. Write an *E* next to those things that are external motivators and an *I* next to those things that are internal motivators. Do you have more *E*s or *I*s? Does this match the activity you just completed?

4. Why do you think they matched or did not match? Write a paragraph explaining your answer.
Student answers will vary.
_____
_____
_____
_____

Name _____ Date _____ Period _____

CHAPTER 5: Ethics and Social Responsibility

Part 1: Check Your Knowledge

Matching

Write the correct term for each definition on the line provided.

Key Terms

code of conduct
code of ethics
copyright
corporate culture
corporate social responsibility
customer relationship management (CRM)
cyber bullying
ethics
Environmental Protection Agency (EPA)
false advertising
Federal Trade Commission (FTC)
freeware
goodwill
netiquette
philanthropy
phishing
Sarbanes-Oxley Act
shareware
social responsibility
software piracy
spam

1. The illegal copying or downloading of software.
   software piracy

2. Electronic messages sent in bulk to people who did not give a company permission to e-mail them.
   spam

3. Fully functional software that can be used forever without purchasing it.
   freeware

4. The federal agency that provides information about environmental-compliance rules and regulations.
   Environmental Protection Agency (EPA)

5. Using the Internet to harass or threaten an individual.
   cyber bullying

Copyright Goodheart-Willcox Co., Inc.   37

6. The law that requires companies to be open and honest in their accounting and reporting practices.
   Sarbanes-Oxley Act

7. Provides general principles or values, often social or moral, that guide an organization.
   code of ethics

8. The main federal agency that enforces advertising laws and regulations.
   Federal Trade Commission (FTC)

9. A system to track contact and other information for current and potential customers.
   customer relationship management (CRM)

10. How the owners and employees of a company think, feel, and act as a business.
    corporate culture

11. The set of rules of behavior based on ideas about what is right and wrong.
    ethics

12. The exclusive right to copy, license, sell, or distribute material.
    copyright

13. Overstating the features and benefits of products or services or making false claims about them.
    false advertising

14. The accepted social and professional guidelines for communicating using the Internet.
    netiquette

15. The advantage a business has due to its good reputation.
    goodwill

16. Promoting the welfare of others—usually through volunteering, protecting resources, or donating money or products.
    philanthropy

17. The actions a business takes to further social good.
    corporate social responsibility

18. Copyrighted software that is available free of charge on a trial basis, then must be purchased for continued use.
    shareware

19. Behaving with sensitivity to social, environmental, and economic issues.
    social responsibility

20. Lists specific behaviors expected from employees representing the company in business situations.
    code of conduct

Chapter 5   Ethics and Social Responsibility

Name _____

True or False

Decide whether each statement is true or false and enter *T* or *F* on the line provided. If the statement is false, rewrite the statement to make it true.

1. Ethics are not always vital to the success of most businesses. False. For anyone in business, ethics are vital to their success.

2. From the Industrial Revolution in the 18th century until recently, business had a reputation for a lack of ethics. True

3. In companies that take ethics seriously, top management will project the value system that drives behavior. True

4. In 1962, President John F. Kennedy addressed the Congress and outlined four basic consumer rights. To this day, there are still only four basic consumer rights. False: Since 1962, four more consumer rights have been added to the original four.

5. If an action is legal, it is always ethical. False. The line between legal and ethical can be very thin. Sometime an act can be legal, but unethical.

6. Marketers who misrepresent their products or services risk losing customers. True

7. There are very strict rules and regulations for businesses that produce consumer products. True

8. In the United States, a copyright statement is required for original work. False. In the United States, an original work is copyrighted as soon as it is in tangible form. A copyright statement is not required.

9. Customers have the right to expect a company to keep their information confidential. True

10. Internet access provided by the company can be used for business and personal purposes. False. Internet access provided by the company should be used only for business purposes.

Part 2: Marketing by the Numbers

Charity Marketing

Many businesses engage in the practice known as *charity marketing*. Charity marketing is a business partnering with a local nonprofit organization to help with fund raising while marketing the business' products and services to the charitable organization's members. Many charities understand that a business is looking for a return on its investment. However, the business must keep in mind that the major goal of charity marketing is helping the charity.

In this scenario, the city food pantry partners with a local restaurant to raise money for food baskets to be distributed during the holiday season. The restaurant decided to give 30% of its sales each Wednesday evening during October, November, and the first week in December to the food pantry to help with the cost of the food baskets.

The following table shows the Wednesday sales during October and November. Calculate the amount the restaurant has agreed to donate. Next, calculate the total the amount of money donated during that time to the food pantry. Round your answer to the nearest cent and then write your answers in the last column of the table.

		Total Sales for the Day	Donation Amount
1.	Wednesday #1	$573.65	$ 172.10
2.	Wednesday #2	$894.52	$ 268.36
3.	Wednesday #3	$781.35	$ 234.41
4.	Wednesday #4	$698.90	$ 209.67
5.	Wednesday #5	$745.27	$ 248.42
6.	Wednesday #6	$777.82	$ 233.35
7.	Wednesday #7	$710.04	$ 213.01
8.	Wednesday #8	$839.53	$ 251.86
9.	Wednesday #9	$981.15	$ 294.35
10.		Total	$2,125.53

Chapter 5   Ethics and Social Responsibility   41

Name _____

Part 3: Demonstrate Your Knowledge

Social Responsibility

The following statements describe actions by various businesses. Determine whether the actions are socially responsible or not. Justify your answers using complete sentences in the space provided.

1. Bright Morning Greeting Cards uses recycled paper for its greeting cards.
   Student answers will vary.

2. A discount chain store does *not* promote women to management positions.
   Student answers will vary.

3. A local supermarket suggests that customers round up their bills to the nearest dollar. For example, if a total bill was $40.36, the customer would pay $41.00. The store then matches the extra amounts and donates the total to a homeless shelter.
   Student answers will vary.

4. A restaurant discriminates against some customers by *not* seating them promptly, even when there are open tables.
   Student answers will vary.

5. Avon, Aveda, and other cosmetic companies do *not* test their products on animals.
   Student answers will vary.

6. Newman's Own, a manufacturer of pasta sauces and other food products, contributes all after-tax profits to charity, over $350 million to date.
   Student answers will vary.

Copyright Goodheart-Willcox Co., Inc.

7. A company is doing very well and pays its employees fairly. It does *not* contribute to any charities or involve its employees in any community activities.

   Student answers will vary.

8. A company purchases safety equipment but does *not* train employees on how to use it.

   Student answers will vary.

9. A manufacturing company's processes emit air pollution; however, it does nothing to reduce the pollution.

   Student answers will vary.

10. A company develops a toy that has a potential choking hazard for children.

    Student answers will vary.

Chapter 5 Ethics and Social Responsibility 43

Name _____

Part 4: Be Your Own Leader

Building a Team

Deiondre was recently elected as President of her CTSO. As president, she is responsible for organizing meetings, creating meeting agendas, and running the meetings. She must also make sure that the officers and members complete the work the group has decided to do. That work includes three fundraisers, a community event to raise awareness for victims of violence, and an upcoming conference. There are a total of eight officers, including herself, on the team. The officers include a vice-president, secretary, treasurer, historian, and three class representatives.

Over the past several weeks, Deiondre has observed that the officers are not working well together. The last fundraiser did not go well, and Deiondre chose not to attend. Officers seem to want to assign responsibility for the failed fundraiser to others. Additionally, a few of the officers are failing to complete their work assignments, which is causing resentment among those officers picking up the slack.

At the last meeting, three of the officers presented Deiondre with the following letter.

Dear Deiondre:

> As you may have noticed, the officer meetings are spent talking about old issues and not about accomplishing our goals. You are not running the meetings well. For example, last week Caleb and Dominque spent most of the meeting talking to each other and asked you what the problem was when you asked them to pay attention. Additionally, the fundraiser did not work because the officers in charge waited until the last minute to organize it, and you don't call meetings until the last minute. We have not had an agenda for the last two meetings and feel like we are wasting our time. This needs to be discussed at our next meeting, and we recommend that you consider resigning as president to allow someone with better organizational skills to run our 200-member chapter.

Respectfully,

Westley, Emily, and Sarah

Deiondre is determined that she will bring the team around. She has no plans to resign, but needs your help in deciding what to do in the short- and long-terms in order to get her chapter officers back on the right course.

Answer the following questions and be prepared to discuss them in class.

1. What do you think are two main issues that Deiondre needs to immediately address with the team?

   Student answers will vary.

   _____

   _____

2. Create a short-term plan for Deiondre. What are two or three things that she can do in the next two weeks to repair the damage and begin to build a cohesive and effective team of officers?

   Student answers will vary.

   _____

   _____

Copyright Goodheart-Willcox Co., Inc.

3. Create a long-term plan for Deiondre. What are two or three things she could do in the next semester to continue developing camaraderie and cohesiveness in the team?

   Student answers will vary.

4. As a leader, what would you have done differently in the beginning to develop a cohesive team that would work more effectively together?

   Student answers will vary.

Name _____ Date _____ Period _____

CHAPTER 6
Economic Principles and Systems

Part 1: Check Your Knowledge

Matching

Write the letter of the correct answer next to each definition on the line provided.

Key Terms

capital
capital good
command economy
economic input
economic output
economics
economic system
entrepreneurship
factor of production
infrastructure
labor
land
market economy
mixed economy
natural resource
opportunity cost
productivity
scarcity
social democracy
supply and demand
technology
traditional economy

1. The economic principle relating the quantity of products available to meet consumer demand.
   supply and demand

2. The amount of work a person can do in a specific amount of time.
   productivity

3. All of the tools and machinery used to produce goods or provide services.
   capital

4. The work performed by people in businesses.
   labor

5. Consists of the transportation systems and utilities necessary for a modern economy.
   infrastructure

Copyright Goodheart-Willcox Co., Inc.

45

6. Both the government and individuals are involved in making economic resource decisions.
   mixed economy

7. Raw material found in nature, such as soil, water, minerals, plants, and animals.
   natural resource

8. The value of the best option you did not choose.
   opportunity cost

9. A socialist system of government achieved by democratic means.
   social democracy

10. The economic resource a nation uses to make products and supply services for their citizens.
    factor of production

11. The science that deals with examining how goods and services are produced, sold, and used.
    economics

12. The use of science to invent useful things or to solve problems.
    technology

13. All the goods and services produced by an economic system during a specific time.
    economic output

14. An economy in which the government makes all of the economic decisions.
    command economy

15. All of a nation's natural resources.
    land

16. The willingness and ability to start a new business.
    entrepreneurship

17. An economy in which most citizens have just enough to survive.
    traditional economy

18. Includes the resources used to make products.
    economic input

19. An organized way in which a state or nation allocates its resources to create goods and services.
    economic system

20. Occurs when demand is higher than the available resources.
    scarcity

Chapter 6   Economic Principles and Systems

47

Name _____

True or False

Decide whether each statement is true or false and enter *T* or *F* on the line provided. If the statement is false, rewrite the statement to make it true.

1. One quality of a resource is that it can only be used once. True

2. Economic decisions often have more than two options. True

3. The factors of production are land, labor, capital, and partnerships. False. The factors of production are land, labor, capital, and entrepreneurship.

4. Every good produced uses natural resources in some form. True

5. Capital goods are those products businesses use to sell to consumers. False. Capital goods are those products businesses use to produce other goods, rather than being bought by consumers.

6. Economic input is all the goods and services produced by an economic system during a specific time. False. Economic output is all the goods and services produced by an economic system during a specific time.

7. A nation's economic system develops around the way it deals with scarcity. True

8. Command economies are associated with two related political philosophies: communism and free enterprise. False. Command economies are associated with two related political philosophies: communism and socialism.

9. A market economy is one in which individuals are not free to make their own economic decisions. False. A market economy is one in which individuals are free to make their own economic decisions.

10. In a mixed economy, both the government and individuals make decisions about economic resource. True

Copyright Goodheart-Willcox Co., Inc.

Open Response

Write your response to each of the following statements or questions in the space provided. Use complete sentences.

1. When the Berlin Wall came down, Otto and Judith moved west to get higher paying jobs. After a few months, they missed the way they used to live. "Life is too hard now," Otto said. "The jobs are very competitive, and we must work longer and harder than before. Everything is expensive. When we need something, we pay or go without." Judith adds, "Before, our living conditions weren't very nice, but life was easier. The government provided jobs, housing, and medical care for us. Here, you have to search and compete for everything." Which type of economy were Otto and Judith used to? Give evidence from the paragraph to support your answer.

   Student answers will vary.

2. Nikolai's grandparents, Oleksandr and Ella, live in a government-owned building. They receive a pension that covers their living expenses, and they have free health care. They live on the ninth floor. Even though Oleksandr and Ella cannot climb stairs, the elevator makes it easy to get to their floor. However, when the elevator breaks down, they are stranded in their apartments for weeks or even a month. If they are lucky, a neighbor might bring them a loaf of bread. Nikolai's father wants his parents to join him in the United States, but they would lose their pensions. Oleksandr and Ella do not want to be a burden to their son and his family. In which type of economy do Oleksandr and Ella live? Give evidence from the paragraph to support your answer.

   Student answers will vary.

3. Jamal and his father, Franklin, have a painting and wallpapering business. They have completed many residential and commercial projects for Shawna, Jamal's sister, who is a successful interior decorator. Shawna's clients like that she takes care of the painting and wallpapering because the results are always excellent. Much of her success depends on the excellent work of her father and brother. So, Shawna has suggested they to go into business together. They agreed. Now a lawyer is drawing up the incorporation papers. In which type of economy do Jamal, Franklin, and Shawna live? Give evidence from the paragraph to support your answer.

   Student answers will vary.

Chapter 6   Economic Principles and Systems 49

Name _____

4. Like most people in their country, Duong and his mother are poor. When he was eight, Duong went to live on the streets so he would not be a burden to his mother. His future was bleak. Ten years later, when he was a teenager, a social worker taught Duong to make exquisite little boxes and candleholders. Now, a nonprofit export company helps Duong sell his work in other countries. Duong now supports both himself and his mother. What type of economy did Duong probably live in when he was young? Which type of economy is he living in now? Give evidence from the paragraph to support your answer.

Student answers will vary. _____

_____

_____

5. Anna is the mother of twins. For two years after her children were born, she was able to stay home with them while receiving close to her full income from the government. Now, she is back teaching physics at a local college. Each morning, she leaves her toddlers at the fine childcare center in her neighborhood. Anna pays nothing for her children's care, but like others in her country, she and her husband pay a high rate of taxes. In which type of economy do Anna and her family live in? Give evidence from the paragraph to support your answer.

Student answers will vary. _____

_____

Part 2: Marketing by the Numbers

Rounding Numbers in Marketing

Many marketing activities involve the use of large numbers. In many situations, exact numbers are important. However, a marketer also needs to know how to round numbers and when to round them.

Rounding a number means to take an exact number and replace it with another number that is close to it in value, but is easier or more useful to work with. Rounded numbers tend to end in zero. For example, the US population estimate for January, 2013 was 315,120,164. This number is an estimate because the population is always changing. For that reason, an exact number is never completely accurate. As a result, when speaking about population, a rounded number is often more useful. If the US population number was rounded to the nearest hundred million, it would be 300,000,000. If rounding to the nearest hundred thousand, the answer is 315,000,000.

Complete the following rounding chart for the number 503,824,373. This number is the population estimate of the European Union for July, 2012.

Round to Place Value	Rounded Number
Tens	503,824,370
Hundreds	503,824,400
Thousands	503,824,000
Ten Thousands	503,820,000
Hundred Thousands	503,800,000
Millions	504,000,000
Ten Millions	500,000,000
Hundred Millions	500,000,000

Chapter 6   Economic Principles and Systems   51

Name _____

Part 3: Demonstrate Your Knowledge

Economic Input and Output

Read the following article. After you have finished, you will be asked to give examples of the various B2B and B2C transactions that occurred in the narrative.

Americans love sandwiches. The nationwide favorite is the ham sandwich followed by the BLT. However, there are also regional favorites, such as tacos in the Southwest, the shrimp po'boy in New Orleans, the grilled Cuban sandwich in Miami, and the lobster roll in Maine. In Philadelphia, it's the cheesesteak, the city's signature sandwich.

The sandwiches at Mike's Philly Cheesesteak begin with long loaves of bread, delivered by a local bakery every morning. The steak is beef imported from New Zealand and Australia. The other sandwich ingredients are olive oil, oregano, onions grown on nearby farms, and cheeses—American, cheddar, or provolone.

Sandwiches are made to order, but Mike's employees do a lot of preparation before the busy lunch and dinner hours. They use a heavy-duty mechanical chopper for the onions and feed the beef through an electric slicer. They shred each cheese in another machine and put each type in a separate pot to be melted, as needed. The ingredients are stored in huge refrigerators.

Gas grills are turned on every morning and kept going until midnight. Cooks grill the onions ahead of time and keep them hot. The meat is grilled when each sandwich is ordered.

Customers can order a sandwich as *with* or *without* (onions) and name the desired type of cheese. A cook then puts thinly sliced steak on the hot grill with olive oil and oregano. As the meat sizzles, the employee cuts a length of bread and splits it in half. After the steak is grilled, it is piled on the bread, topped with a big spoonful of onions and a ladle of melted cheese, and capped with the other half of the bread. The finished sandwich is wrapped in white paper and handed to the customer.

Started by one man, Mike's has good food and a convenient location—downtown on a busy street near the subway and bus lines. Customers feel safe lining up at Mike's, even at night, due to regular police patrol and streetlights that keep the area bright. Mike's takes phone and e-mail orders and accepts credit card payments for $20 or more.

1. Give an example of customer satisfaction as described above.
   Student answers will vary.
   _____

2. What else could Mike do to improve customer satisfaction?
   Student answers will vary.
   _____

3. What are Mike's economic inputs in land?
   Student answers will vary.
   _____

Copyright Goodheart-Willcox Co., Inc.

4. What are Mike's economic inputs in labor?
   Student answers will vary.

5. What are Mike's economic inputs in capital goods?
   Student answers will vary.

6. What are Mike's economic inputs in capital infrastructure?
   Student answers will vary.

7. What are Mike's economic inputs in capital technology?
   Student answers will vary.

8. What is Mike's economic output?
   Student answers will vary.

Chapter 6 Economic Principles and Systems

Name _____

Part 4: Be Your Own Leader

Social and Ethical Responsibility

Most companies are socially responsible and ethical. However, some are not. For this activity, identify one socially and/or ethically responsible company and one company that has acted unethically or socially irresponsible at some point in time.

1. Identify the company and the owner or CEO of the company that is socially *or* ethically responsible.

    Name of company:_____

    Name of owner or CEO:_____

2. Describe the company and what they do to be socially *or* ethically responsible.

    Student answers will vary.

    _____

    _____

3. Describe how the owner or CEO, as leader of the organization, influenced the company to be socially and ethically responsible.

    Student answers will vary.

    _____

    _____

4. Identify the company and the owner or CEO that was socially *or* ethically irresponsible.

    Name of company:_____

    Name of owner or CEO:_____

5. Describe the company and what it did that was socially *or* ethically irresponsible.

    Student answers will vary.

    _____

    _____

6. Summarize why you think the first company acted responsibly and the second company did not. Write a paragraph making sure to use complete sentences.

    Student answers will vary.

    _____

    _____

Copyright Goodheart-Willcox Co., Inc.

7. Write a one- or two-page paper summarizing what you learned about the social and ethical responsibility of business leaders. In your paper, describe how, as a leader, you would act socially and ethically responsible in your future marketing career.

Student answers will vary.

Name _____ Date _____ Period _____

CHAPTER 7
Market Forces and Economic Indicators

Part 1: Check Your Knowledge

Matching

Write the correct term for each definition on the line provided.

Key Terms

consumer price index (CPI)
cost-push inflation
demand-pull inflation
economic growth rate
equilibrium
full employment
gross domestic product (GDP)
indicator
inflation
inflation rate
labor force
law of supply and demand
market demand
market supply
nominal GDP
nonprice competition
per capita GDP
profit motive
real GDP
specialization
standard of living
stock
stock market
stock market index
unemployment rate

1. Shows the general direction of growth for the overall economy.
   economic growth rate

2. The GDP of a nation divided by its population.
   per capita GDP

3. A sign that shows the condition or existence of something.
   indicator

4. The market value of all final products produced in a country during specific time period.
   gross domestic product (GDP)

5. Type of inflation occurring when increased demand pulls up prices.
   demand-pull inflation

Copyright Goodheart-Willcox Co., Inc.

6. The financial well being of the average person in a country.
   standard of living

7. The term for a general rise in prices throughout the economy.
   inflation

8. The GDP in current dollars, having been calculated without an adjustment for inflation.
   nominal GDP

9. Type of inflation occurring when increased business costs push up production costs and consumer prices.
   cost-push inflation

10. The total demand of every person willing and able to buy a product.
    market demand

11. The rate of change of prices calculated on a monthly or yearly basis.
    inflation rate

12. A measure of the average change in the prices paid by urban consumers for typical consumer goods and services over time.
    consumer price index (CPI)

13. The percentage of the civilian labor force that is unemployed.
    unemployment rate

14. The GDP in constant dollars, having been calculated with an adjustment for inflation.
    real GDP

15. Comprised of all people who are capable of working and who want to work.
    labor force

16. Would occur if every person who is willing and able to work had a job.
    full employment

17. A system for buying and selling stocks or a place where stocks are bought and sold.
    stock market

18. The total supply of every seller willing and able to sell a product.
    market supply

19. Economic principle that both the supply and the demand of a product affects its price.
    law of supply and demand

20. A way other than price to win business.
    nonprice competition

21. When business owners earn profits and are motivated to start and expand businesses.
    profit motive

Chapter 7   Market Forces and Economic Indicators

57

Name _____

22. Represents the right of ownership in a corporation.
    stock

23. Assigning a worker or group of workers to a specialized task for increased efficiency.
    specialization

24. The point at which the supply equals the demand for a product.
    equilibrium

True or False

Decide whether each statement is true or false and enter T or F on the line provided. If the statement is false, rewrite the statement to make it true.

1. Supply is the quantity of goods that consumers want to purchase. False. Demand is the quantity of goods that consumers want to purchase.

2. Generally, high demand raises prices, while low demand decreases prices. True

3. One of the major roles of marketing is to increase demand through promotion. True

4. Marketing does not help to increase sales simply by developing programs to attract new customers. False. Marketing can help to increase sales by developing programs to attract new customers.

5. When economic indicators are normal, the economy is doing well. True

6. The most widely followed indicators of the economy are gross domestic product (GDP) and per capita GDP. False. The most widely followed indicators of the economy are gross domestic product (GDP), per capita GDP, inflation rate, and the unemployment rate.

7. The major spenders in the US economy are businesses. False. The major spenders in the US economy are consumers.

8. The larger the percentage rate of change, the faster the economy is changing—for better or worse. True

9. If the price of only one product rises, it does not necessarily indicate inflation. True

10. The United States has experienced hyperinflation only on a few occasions. False. The United States has never experienced hyperinflation.

Copyright Goodheart-Willcox Co., Inc.

Part 2: Marketing by the Numbers

Billions and Trillions

National economies and large corporations deal with huge sums of money, amounts in the billions and trillions. Reading these numbers accurately is important.

Place Value Chart											
Trillions Group			,	Billions Group			,	Millions Group			,	Thousands Group			,	Units Group			Decimal .
4	2	7	,	1	0	6	,	9	5	2	,	0	0	0	,	0	0	0	.

To figure out which place group a number is in, start counting places from the decimal point and move left. The three places to the left of the decimal are the units group. Places 4 through 6 are the thousands group. Places 7 through 9 are the millions group. Places 10 through 12 are the billions group. Places 13 through 15 are the trillions group.

Have you heard someone say, "Pat is earning over seven figures"? How much is this person earning? Seven figures refers to the seven places in the place value chart. The person is earning over a million dollars. Someone else is earning in the high six figures. How much is this person earning? Over $500,000 (five hundred thousand dollars).

Remember that each place value group is read as a three-digit number, and then the name of the group is added. Remember also the role of zero as a place holder. The number in the chart above **427,106,952,000,000** is read as follows:

four hundred twenty-seven trillion, one hundred six billion, nine hundred fifty-two million.

The National Retail Federation published the annual estimated sales for general merchandise retailers in the year 2010 as shown in the following chart. Convert the numbers in the second column to their full numbers and place those numbers into the third column. The first category, General Merchandise, is done for you as an example.

Category	2010 Annual Sales in Millions of Dollars	Converted 2010 Annual Sales
General Merchandise	610,279	610,279,000,000
1. Health and Personal Care	263,960	263,960,000,000
2. Department Stores	186,604	186,604,000,000
3. Shoe Stores	27,556	27,557,000,000
4. Nonstore Retailers	361,328	361,328,000,000
5. Book Stores	16,497	16,497,000,000
6. Family Clothing Stores	84,899	84,899,000,000
7. Miscellaneous Store Retailers	120,081	120,081,000,000
8. Electronic Shopping and Mail Order Houses	272,215	272,215,000,000
9. Home Furnishing Stores	41,831	41,831,000,000
10. Sporting Goods	40,209	40,209,000,000

Chapter 7   Market Forces and Economic Indicators

Name _____

Write the numbers from the third column into the place value chart that follows.

Number	Trillions	,	Billions	,	Millions	,	Thousands	,	Units
1			2 6 3		9 6 0		0 0 0		0 0 0
2			1 8 6		6 0 4		0 0 0		0 0 0
3			2 7		5 5 7		0 0 0		0 0 0
4			3 6 1		3 2 8		0 0 0		0 0 0
5			1 6		4 9 7		0 0 0		0 0 0
6			8 4		8 9 9		0 0 0		0 0 0
7			1 2 0		0 8 1		0 0 0		0 0 0
8			2 7 2		2 1 5		0 0 0		0 0 0
9			4 1		8 3 1		0 0 0		0 0 0
10			4 0		2 0 9		0 0 0		0 0 0

Place Value Chart for Estimated Sales, 2010, in Dollars

Copyright Goodheart-Willcox Co., Inc.

Part 3: Demonstrate Your Knowledge

Supply and Demand

Supply and demand for products would be easy to predict in a constant environment. However, the environment is rarely constant. Market forces that can affect supply and demand include marketing, economic environment, and social trends. Depending on the existing market forces, it is harder to predict whether supply or demand will rise or fall. Read each paragraph and answer the questions in the spaces provided.

A TV advertisement features groups of people laughing as they gallop their horses along a white-sand beach. One person turns to the camera and says, "I had no idea that travel would be so much fun!" The voice-over says, "Don't miss out on the fun you could be having. Call a travel agent today."

1. What kind of product is being advertised?

    Travel agency services

2. This is an example of which market force?

    Marketing

3. How might this ad affect demand?

    Increase

Crystal and Lloyd have two children. Before the children were born, Crystal worked as the office manager for a large real estate firm. For several years after her children were born, Lloyd was a stay-at-home dad. However, prices started rising, and Crystal's income could no longer support everything that the family wanted and needed. Lloyd returned to work at a job similar to his old one.

4. What changed in Lloyd's situation?

    The family's economic situation

5. What caused the change?

    Changes in the economy

How might the demand of a product change if a large number of unemployed workers returned to the workforce? Read the following list of products and services. Next to each one, indicate whether you think demand would rise or fall if more workers returned to the workforce.

Product	Demand Rise or Fall?	Why?
Cars and car care	Rise	Employed workers driving more
Cell phones	Rise	Buying more for self and children
Child care	Rise	Need child care while at work
Dry cleaners	Rise	Business clothes need dry cleaning
Home canning supplies	Fall	Less time for canning
Home cleaning services	Rise	Less time for cleaning
Home security system	Rise	No one home during the day
Restaurant meals	Rise	Less time to cook

Chapter 7 Market Forces and Economic Indicators

Name _____

Part 4: Leadership

Leaders Present

If you are going to be a leader, you have to be willing to stand up for what you believe in. Whether you are having a one-to-one conversation with another person or presenting to a group, it is important for leaders to be good communicators. Good communication takes practice. For this activity, you will plan and create a five-minute presentation on a leadership topic. Check with your instructor to see if you can present with another person or if you will present on your own.

First, brainstorm on where you could make the presentation. Presenting to your classmates is easy. Think outside the box. Could you present what you have learned about leadership to another class, to the administration, the school board, a community group, your coworkers, your sports team, etc.? Make a list of three groups to whom you could present. Get approval from your instructor to interview the groups.

1. Groups I could present to

   a. _Student answers will vary._____

   b. _____

   c. _____

2. Topic of Presentation

   _Student answers will vary._____

Presentation Outline

3. Opening _Student answers will vary._____

   _____

   _____

   _____

4. Key Points _Student answers will vary._____

   _____

   _____

   _____

5. Summary _Student answers will vary._____

   _____

   _____

   _____

Copyright Goodheart-Willcox Co., Inc.

6. Media to be used (electronic slide show, video, etc.)—attach a copy, if appropriate.

   Student answers will vary.

Self-Reflection on Presentation

7. Summary Student answers will vary.

8. What went well? Student answers will vary.

9. What could be improved? Student answers will vary.

Name _____ Date _____ Period _____

Chapter 8: Business Cycles and the Role of Government

Part 1: Check Your Knowledge

Matching

Write the correct term for each definition on the line provided.

Key Terms

business cycle
coincident indicator
depression
economic recovery
expansion
externality
fiscal policy
lagging indicator
leading indicator
laissez-faire
monetary policy
peak
recession
trough

1. A period of great decline in total output, employment, trade, and income.
   recession

2. Changes after a change in economic activity.
   lagging indicator

3. A period when GDP is rising.
   expansion

4. Regulating the money supply and interest rates by a central bank.
   monetary policy

5. The lowest stage of a business cycle that marks the end of a recession.
   trough

6. Consists of alternating periods of expansion and contraction in the economy.
   business cycle

7. The economic policy allowing businesses to operate with very little interference from the government.
   laissez-faire

8. The highest point in a business cycle.
   peak

9. Something that affects people not directly connected to an economic activity.
   externality

10. An economic contraction that is very severe and long lasting.
    depression

Chapter 8 Business Cycles and the Role of Government

65

Name _____

True or False

Decide whether each statement is true or false and enter *T* or *F* on the line provided. If the statement is false, rewrite the statement to make it true.

1. The GDP does *not* grow at the same rate every year. True

2. US business cycles rarely repeat. False. US business cycles repeat over many years.

3. An economic recovery is the period of expansion before a trough. False. An economic recovery is the period of expansion after a trough.

4. Fiscal policy is the tax and spending decisions made by the President and Congress. True

5. A leading indicator is one that changes after a change in economic activity. False. A leading indicator is one that changes before a change in economic activity.

6. A coincident indicator is one that changes at the same time as changes in economic activity. True

7. Changing stock prices reflect expectations for changes in economic activity. True

8. When writing the US Constitution, the founding fathers gave Congress sweeping economic powers. False. When writing the US Constitution, the founding fathers gave Congress limited economic powers.

9. Often, the federal government uses fiscal policy to smooth business cycles and lessen the impact of recessions. True

10. When the economy is slowing, the Fed can use different economic tools to increase the money supply and help lower interest rates. True

Part 2: Marketing by the Numbers

Gross Domestic Product (GDP)

The GDPs for the years 2003 through 2011 are listed in the table that follows.

Year	Gross Domestic Product (in dollars)	Growth Rate of the Economy (from the previous year)
2003	10.886 trillion	N/A
2004	11.607 trillion	6.623%
2005	12.347 trillion	6.375%
2006	13.120 trillion	6.261%
2007	13.743 trillion	4.748%
2008	14.292 trillion	3.994%
2009	13.864 trillion	2.994%
2010	14.447 trillion	4.205%
2011	15.094 trillion	4.478%

You can tell how fast an economy is growing by calculating the *growth rate of the economy*. Use the following formula and the data in the previous table to help you fill in the last column. Round percents to the nearest thousandth.

$$\frac{(\text{GDP for Time 2} - \text{GDP for Time 1}) \times 100}{\text{GDP for Time 1}} = \text{Growth Rate of the Economy}$$

1. Find the growth rate of the economy from 2003 to 2004.
   Time 1 = 2003
   Time 2 = 2004
   GDP for Time 1 = __10.886__
   GDP for Time 2 = __11.607__

2. Find the growth rate of the economy from 2004 to 2005.
   Time 1 = 2004
   Time 2 = 2005
   GDP for Time 1 = __11.607__
   GDP for Time 2 = __12.347__

3. Find the growth rate of the economy from 2005 to 2006.
   Time 1 = 2005
   Time 2 = 2006
   GDP for Time 1 = __12.347__
   GDP for Time 2 = __13.120__

4. Find the growth rate of the economy from 2006 to 2007.
   Time 1 = 2006
   Time 2 = 2007
   GDP for Time 1 = __13.120__
   GDP for Time 2 = __13.743__

Chapter 8   Business Cycles and the Role of Government

Name _____

5. Find the growth rate of the economy from 2007 to 2008.
   Time 1 = 2007
   Time 2 = 2008
   GDP for Time 1 = 13.743
   GDP for Time 2 = 14.292

6. Find the growth rate of the economy from 2008 to 2009.
   Time 1 = 2008
   Time 2 = 2009
   GDP for Time 2 = 14.292
   GDP for Time 1 = 13.864

7. Find the growth rate of the economy from 2009 to 2010.
   Time 1 = 2009
   Time 2 = 2010
   GDP for Time 1 = 13.864
   GDP for Time 2 = 14.447

8. Find the growth rate of the economy from 2010 to 2011.
   Time 1 = 2010
   Time 2 = 2011
   GDP for Time 1 = 14.447
   GDP Time 2 = 15.094

9. Between which years was the growth rate of the economy the greatest? Between 2003 and 2004; it went up by 6.623%

10. Between which years was the growth rate of the economy the least? Between 2008 and 2009; it went down 2.994%.

Calculations

Can you imagine how big a trillion is? Here is an exercise to help you imagine it. Suppose someone gives you $500 a day until you have a total of $10,000. How many days would it take? The answer is 20 days. To arrive at this answer, you know the total amount received is $10,000. You also know that you will be given $500 a day. To find out how many days it would take to get $10,000, divide the total amount received ($10,000) by the daily amount received ($500)—or 10,000 ÷ 500 = 20. Therefore, it would take you 20 days, or nearly three weeks, to accumulate $10,000. Use the information in this paragraph to answer the following questions. You may use a calculator. Along with the correct answers, show your work.

1. How many days would it take to accumulate $100,000?

   200 days

   100,000 ÷ 500 = 200

2. How many months is this?

   6.7 months

   200 ÷ 30 = 6.7

Copyright Goodheart-Willcox Co., Inc.

3. How many days would it take to accumulate $1 million?

   2,000 days

   1,000,000 ÷ 500 = 2,000

4. How many months would it take to accumulate $1 million?

   66.67 months

   2,000 ÷ 30 = 66.67

5. How many years is this?

   5.56 years

   66.67 ÷ 12 = 5.56

6. How many days would it take to accumulate $1 billion?

   2,000,000 (million) days

   1,000,000,000 ÷ 500 = 2,000,000

7. How many months would it take to accumulate $1 billion?

   66,666.67 months

   2,000,000 ÷ 30 = 66,666.67

8. How many years is this?

   5,555.56 years

   66,666.67 ÷ 12 = 5,555.56

9. How many days would it take to accumulate $1 trillion?

   2,000,000,000 (billion) days

   1,000,000,000,000 ÷ 500 = 2,000,000,000

10. How many years is this?

    5,555,555.56 (5.6 million) years

    2,000,000,000 ÷ 30 = 66,666,666.67 months

    66,666,666.67 months ÷ 12 = 5,555,555.56 years

Chapter 8   Business Cycles and the Role of Government

Name _____

Part 3: Demonstrate Your Knowledge

Market Forces

Market forces can directly affect an economy, and there is still ongoing pressure for the government to be involved in the economy. Complete the following chart. In the second column, write the reason for the listed market weakness. In the third column, give an example of what the government could do to counteract that weakness. Sample answers appear below.

Market Weakness and Government Response		
Market Weakness	**Reason**	**What Government Can Do to Counteract the Weakness**
Need for quick profits	A business risks failing if it is unable to make a profit in a reasonably short time.	Through taxes, government can support long-term projects that individual business cannot afford, such as scientific research. Government can also provide products that do not fit into the market economy: public goods and services, such as roads, national defense, and public education.
No safety net in poor economic times	The free-market system is based on the ability to pay, regardless of illness, natural disaster, mental or physical disability, economic downturns.	Through taxes, the government can provide a safety net through programs such as Social Security, disaster relief, and unemployment compensation.

Read the paragraph and answer the questions that follow.

During colonial times in America, fire was a major hazard. Householders fought fires on their own or relied on their neighbors for help. In 1736, Benjamin Franklin organized the first group of volunteer firefighters in Philadelphia. A few years later, he started the first fire insurance company. When fire insurance was purchased for a house, the owner was given a metal marker to put on the front of the house. Other fire insurance companies formed, and each issued its own metal marker. You could walk down the street and see which houses were insured by which companies. You could also see which houses were not insured at all.

1. In what ways were the fire insurance companies an example of a market economy?
   Student answers will vary.
   _____
   _____

2. Why did firefighting become a public service provided by local governments?
   Student answers will vary.
   _____
   _____

3. List five public goods or services that you rely on every day.
   Student answers will vary.
   _____
   _____

Copyright Goodheart-Willcox Co., Inc.

Part 4: Be Your Own Leader

Leaders on a Top Secret Mission

On December 6, 2011, a woman walked into a Michigan K-Mart and paid off someone else's layaway just in time for the holidays. That one act of kindness, completed in total secrecy, has taken on a life of its own. People have gone into stores with as much as $20,000 in their hands to anonymously pay off the layaways of others. Leaders give back, and they often do without wanting or needing recognition. A leader will always be willing to recognize others, share in other's successes, and help whenever and wherever they see a need. True leaders will do without expecting anything in return.

As a leader, think of something you could do for someone else. You do not have to spend any money if you do not want to. Giving back is rarely about money. It can be as simple as leaving a note recognizing someone for the work he or she has done.

1. Create your own *secret mission*. Decide what you can do as a leader to give back. Maybe you will volunteer at a local shelter or write a note to all of your teachers and place it in their school mailboxes. There are so many things you could do; narrowing it down to just one thing might be the most difficult part. Fill in the following information about your secret mission.

    Mission title: _Student answers will vary._

    Why I chose this mission: _____

    Why I believe it is important for leaders to give back: _____

    Date(s) of my mission: _____

    Resources I will need: _____

    Others I will need to include for the mission to succeed: _____

2. Once you have completed your mission, complete a self-reflection. Include other ways that, as a leader, you can give back in the future.

    Self-reflection: _Student answers will vary._

    Future thoughts and plans: _____

Name _____ Date _____ Period _____

CHAPTER 9
Global Trade

Part 1: Check Your Knowledge

Matching

Write the correct term for each definition on the line provided.

Key Terms

balance of trade	globalization
currency	import
developed country	multinational corporation
developing country	quota
embargo	tariff
export	trade agreement
floating currency	trade deficit
foreign exchange rate	trade sanction
free-trade zone	trade surplus
global economy	trading bloc

1. Occurs when the exchange rate is set by the supply and demand in the foreign exchange market.
   floating currency

2. Occurs when nations become connected through freely moving goods, labor, and capital across borders.
   globalization

3. A group of countries that join together to trade as if they were one country.
   trading bloc

4. A country with a strong base of industrial production, good infrastructure, and a high standard of living.
   developed country

5. A government order that prohibits trade with a foreign country.
   embargo

Copyright Goodheart-Willcox Co., Inc.

6. An embargo affecting only one or several goods.
   trade sanction

7. A government tax on imported goods.
   tariff

8. Limits the amount of a product imported into a country during a specific period of time.
   quota

9. A document listing the conditions and terms under which goods are imported and exported between countries.
   trade agreement

10. The economic activity of every nation in the world.
    global economy

11. A good that is sold to another country.
    export

12. The cost to convert one currency into another.
    foreign exchange rate

13. Occurs when a nation exports more goods than it imports, which results in a positive balance of trade.
    trade surplus

14. The difference between the exports and imports of a nation.
    balance of trade

15. Produces and sells products in foreign countries as well as inside its borders.
    multinational corporation

16. A country with a lower standard of living, weak infrastructure, and little industry.
    developing country

17. The money that a country uses.
    currency

18. Occurs when a nation imports more goods than it exports, which results in a negative balance of trade.
    trade deficit

Chapter 9 Global Trade

73

Name _____

True or False

Decide whether each statement is true or false and enter *T* or *F* on the line provided. If the statement is false, rewrite the statement to make it true.

1. Sometimes globalization is referred to as international trade. True

2. Natural resources are evenly divided among the nations. False. Natural resources are not evenly divided among the nations.

3. Exports earn money for a country, while imports cost money. True

4. The US annual balance of trade has been a surplus many times. False. The US annual balance of trade has been a surplus only two times.

5. An import is a good that is sold to another country. False. An import is a good that is purchased from another country.

6. When the price of a foreign currency declines, it means the value of a US dollar has strengthened. True

7. Trade sanctions *cannot* prohibit the importation of a specific product for health reasons.
False. Trade sanctions can prohibit the importation of a specific product for health reasons.

8. Before the US government taxed incomes, its main source of revenue was from tariffs.
True

9. Import quotas are designed to protect domestic producers by limiting foreign competition.
True

10. The United States currently has over 300 different trade agreements with other countries.
True

Copyright Goodheart-Willcox Co., Inc.

Part 2: Marketing by the Numbers

Section A

Imagine that you are planning a world tour to the 15 countries listed in the following chart. You start out with 100 US dollars in each country. Using the exchange rates provided, determine how much foreign currency you would receive in each country. Remember to round your numbers to the nearest cent. The first country is completed for you as an example.

Country	Currency	Foreign Units per US Dollar	Foreign Equivalent of 100 US Dollars ($100)
Australia	dollar	0.9465	94.65 Australian dollars
1. Brazil	real	2.0424	204.24 Brazilian reals
2. Canada	dollar	0.9863	98.63 Canadian dollars
3. China	yuan	6.2165	621.65 Chinese yuan
4. Denmark	kroner	5.61	561.00 Danish kroner
5. European Union	euro	0.7527	75.27 euros
6. India	rupee	54.70	5470.00 Indian rupees
7. Japan	yen	88.5650	8,856.50 Japanese yen
8. Mexico	peso	12.6227	1267.27 Mexican pesos
9. Norway	kroner	5.5692	556.92 Norwegian kroner
10. Singapore	dollar	1.22	122.00 Singapore dollars
11. South Africa	rand	8.8064	880.64 South African rands
12. Switzerland	franc	0.9309	93.09 Swiss francs
13. Thailand	baht	29.83	2,983.00 Thai bahts
14. UAE	dirham	3.67	367.00 UAE dirham
15. United Kingdom	pound	0.6250	62.50 UK pounds

Chapter 9   Global Trade

Name _____

Section B

When you leave each country, you have 50 units of that country's currency. Using the exchange rates provided, determine how much you would have in US dollars. Remember to round to the nearest cent. The first country is completed for you as an example. When you have completed the table, answer the questions that follow.

Country	Currency	US Dollars per Unit of Foreign Currency	Exchange Rate Times 50	Equivalent of 50 Foreign Units in US Dollars
Australia	dollar	1.06	52.86	$52.86
1. Brazil	real	0.4901	24.50	$24.50
2. Canada	dollar	1.01	50.68	$50.68
3. China	yuan	0.1607	8.04	$ 8.04
4. Denmark	kroner	0.178	8.90	$ 8.90
5. European Union	euro	1.33	66.46	$66.46
6. India	rupee	0.0183	0.9142	$ 0.91
7. Japan	yen	0.0113	0.5649	$ 0.56
8. Mexico	peso	0.0792	3.96	$ 3.96
9. Norway	kroner	0.1795	8.97	$ 8.97
10. Singapore	dollar	0.8169	40.84	$40.84
11. South Africa	rand	0.1136	5.68	$ 5.68
12. Switzerland	franc	1.07	53.67	$53.67
13. Thailand	baht	0.0335	1.68	$ 1.68
14. UAE	dirham	0.2722	13.61	$13.61
15. United Kingdom	pound	0.0209	80.00	$80.00

16. Which foreign units of currency are worth about a US dime?
    Mexican peso and South African rand

17. Which foreign units of currency are worth about a US quarter?
    UAE dirham

18. Which foreign units of currency are worth about a US dollar?
    Canadian dollar, Singapore dollar, and Swiss franc

19. Which foreign units of currency are worth about a US penny?
    Indian rupee, Thai baht, and UK pound.

20. Which foreign units of currency are worth more than a US dollar?
    European Union euro

Part 3: Demonstrate Your Knowledge

The Kitchen Goes Global

The Kitchen is considering expanding into the emerging markets of Eastern Europe, including some of the countries of the former Soviet Union. Read the following information about *The Kitchen*. Imagine that you are a marketer hired to help the company make some business decisions.

The Kitchen is a successful US business. It offers home-style prepared entrees and side dishes for eating in or as carry out. The business is famous for its rotisserie and oven-roasted chicken. *The Kitchen* also offers a wide variety of fresh vegetables, salads, and breads. Last, but not least, it offers a wide array of family-style desserts. People who do not eat meat have plenty of choices.

The following table shows results from preliminary research completed for the foreign market. Next to each item, write *Plus* if the information indicates the business might be successful. Write *Minus* if the information indicates that the business might have problems.

Preliminary Foreign Market Information	Plus or Minus
1. Usually, both the husband and wife work, so there is little time to cook.	Plus
2. The people like chicken, but they eat more pork. The Kitchen does not currently offer pork dishes.	Minus
3. American culture is popular.	Plus
4. Take-home meals are a new concept.	Minus
5. In the current culture, women always prepare the meals and perform all other household tasks, even if they work full time.	Minus
6. Foreign investment is causing a steady increase in wages.	Plus

7. *The Kitchen* has hired Yuliya, a bookkeeper, who lives in one of the foreign countries the company is considering for expansion. Yuliya works full time and has a husband and three children. Her first responsibility will be to help the business understand its potential customers. List two questions that you want Yuliya to ask potential customers.

   Student answers will vary.

   _____

8. What is the purpose for asking these questions?

   Student answers will vary.

   _____

9. Buying prepared food to bring home is a new concept for the foreign target market. Using complete sentences, list several ways this business could entice consumers to try them.

   Student answers will vary.

   _____

10. A major part of *The Kitchen's* brand is fresh foods. Should the business import chickens, vegetables, and fruits? Explain your answer using complete sentences.

    Student answers will vary.

    _____

Chapter 9 Global Trade

Name _____

Part 4: Be Your Own Leader

Identify Your Strengths and Weaknesses

1. Think about a time when you were in a leadership role. It does not have to be a time when you were labeled as a leader. It could have been as simple as being put in a group for which you assumed the leadership role. Or, as complex as being the captain of a sports team. What did you do to lead others? Did others follow your lead? What did you accomplish?
   Student answers will vary.

2. Think about another time when you were in a leadership role and things did not go well. What happened that caused you *not* be an effective leader?
   Student answers will vary.

Every leader has times when things go very well and other times when they do not. In order to be able to identify what you do well as a leader and how to increase the likelihood of being an effective leader, it is important to identify your strengths and weaknesses as a leader.

3. Complete a SWOT analysis (strengths, weaknesses, opportunities, and threats) in the following chart based on your own experiences as a leader.

A. Strengths—as a leader, what are you good at doing now?	B. Weaknesses—as a leader, what do you need to work on to become more effective?
Student answers will vary.	Student answers will vary.
C. Opportunities—as a leader, what opportunities do you have to showcase your leadership skills or to improve your leadership skills?	D. Threats—as a leader, what things may get in your way?
Student answers will vary.	Student answers will vary.

Copyright Goodheart-Willcox Co., Inc.

4. Write a summary of your leadership SWOT analysis. What did you learn about yourself as a leader by completing the SWOT analysis?

   Student answers will vary.

5. Think of a successful leader in your community. What traits does he or she have that you would like to demonstrate as a leader and why?

   Student answers will vary.

Name _____ Date _____ Period _____

CHAPTER 10
Marketing Research

Part 1: Check Your Knowledge

Matching

Write the correct term for each definition on the line provided.

Key Terms

chamber of commerce
data
database
database marketing
data mining
demographics
demographic trend
diary
fad
focus group
hypothesis
interview
marketing-information system (MkIS)
marketing research
marketing trend
order bias
primary data
product trend
qualitative data
quantitative data
research sample
secondary data
social trend
survey
trade association
trend
variable

1. The pattern of change in consumer behavior that leads to changes in the marketing mix.
   marketing trend

2. The organized system of gathering, sorting, analyzing, evaluating, and distributing information for marketing purposes.
   marketing-information system (MkIS)

3. The pieces of information gained through research.
   data

4. The qualities, such as age, gender, and income, of a specific group of people.
   demographics

Copyright Goodheart-Willcox Co., Inc.

79

5. A written record of the thoughts, activities, or plans of the writer during a given period of time.
   diary

6. Searching through large amounts of digital data to find useful patterns or trends.
   data mining

7. Something that changes or can be changed.
   variable

8. Something that is very popular for a short time and dies out quickly.
   fad

9. A statement that can be tested and proved either true or false.
   hypothesis

10. The skewing of results caused by the order in which questions are placed in a survey.
    order bias

11. An organization of people in a specific type of business or industry.
    trade association

12. An emerging pattern of change.
    trend

13. A group of six to nine people with whom an interview is conducted.
    focus group

14. Provide insight into what people think about a topic.
    qualitative data

15. A change in current product features or a new product being developed.
    product trend

16. Gathering and analyzing information to help make good marketing decisions.
    marketing research

17. Already exists and can be found in a variety of sources.
    secondary data

18. A pattern of change in society.
    social trend

19. A formal meeting between two or more people to obtain certain information.
    interview

20. Change in the size of one segment of the population.
    demographic trend

Chapter 10 Marketing Research **81**

Name _____

21. Pieces of information collected by you or your organization.
primary data

22. The facts and figures from which conclusions can be drawn.
quantitative data

23. Gathering, storing, and using customer data for marketing directly to customers based on their histories.
database marketing

24. Represents the group of people or target market on which the research is done.
research sample

25. A group of businesses whose main purpose is to encourage local business development.
chamber of commerce

True or False

Decide whether each statement is true or false and enter T or F on the line provided. If the statement is false, rewrite the statement to make it true.

1. All good marketing plans refer to the marketing research that helped form the goals, strategies, and tactics. True

2. Research that has *not* yet been analyzed is called raw data. True

3. The key to getting good information through observation is to make sure the subjects know they are being observed. False. The key to getting good information through observation is to make sure the subjects do not know they are being observed.

4. Focus groups are useful for gaining information based on how people in the group interact with each other. True

5. The more trustworthy websites tend to be those ending in *.gov* or *.edu*. True

6. A survey is an organized study in which people are asked different questions. False. A survey is an organized study in which people are asked the same questions.

7. A database is an organized collection of data most often in hardcopies. False. A database is an organized collection of data most often in digital form.

8. The formal research process is very similar to the scientific method. True

9. A hypothesis is always stated in the positive. True

10. Raw data, by itself, is useful. False. Raw data, by itself, is useless.

Chapter 10   Marketing Research

Name _____

Part 2: Marketing by the Numbers

Section A

Numbers shown as percentages are widely used in business and marketing. Economic changes are often reported as percentages. Sales tax is calculated as a percent of the selling price. Business growth is often reported in a percent format. Both primary and secondary data use numbers as percentages to report statistics.

Percents, decimals, and fractions are all related. The same numerical value can be expressed as a fraction, decimal, or in a percent format. For example,

$$½ = 0.5 = 50\%$$

In order to perform calculations with a number in a percent format, it must be turned into a decimal or a fraction. Any percentage can be turned into a fraction with a denominator (the bottom number) of 100. For example,

$$17\% = 17/100$$

Remember that the fraction bar (/) means *divided by* (÷). To turn that fraction into a decimal, divide 17 by 100. An easy way to divide by 100 is to move the decimal point two places to the left:

$$17 ÷ 100 = 0.17$$

To easily turn a number in a percent format into a decimal, remove the percent sign and move the decimal point two places to the left:

$$17\% = 0.17$$

To turn a decimal into a percentage, reverse the process. Move the decimal point two places to the right and add the percent sign. For example,

$$0.29 = 29\%$$

To turn any fraction into a decimal, divide the numerator (the top number) by the denominator (the bottom number). For example, to turn 3/4 into a decimal:

$$3/4 = 0.75$$

(Continued on next page)

Complete the following table by calculating the number of people in each ethnic group by year. Remember to turn the percentage into a decimal. Then, multiply that decimal by the total population for that year. These statistics are from the U.S. Census Bureau.

Year	US Population by Ethnic Group*					Total
	White	Afro-American	Native American	Asian	Other	
1950						
%	89.5	10.0	0.2	0.2	0.1	100
Population (Number)	134,874,138	15,069,736	301,395	301,395	150,697	150,697,361
1960						
%	88.6	10.5	0.3	0.5	0.1	100
Population (Number)	158,880,333	18,828,933	537,970	896,616	179,323	179,323,175
1970						
%	87.5	11.1	0.4	0.8	0.2	100
Population	177,810,435	22,556,524	812,848	1,625,695	406,424	203,211,926
1980						
%	83.1	11.7	0.6	1.5	3.1	100
Population	188,259,564	26,505,859	1,359,275	3,398,187	7,022,920	226,545,805
1990						
%	80.3	12.1	0.8	2.9	3.9	100
Population	199,714,028	30,093,895	1,989,679	7,212,586	9,699,685	248,709,873
2000						
%	75.1	12.3	0.9	3.7	8.0	100
Population	211,347,851	34,614,894	2,532,797	10,412,611	22,513,752	281,421,906
2010						
%	63.7	12.2	.7	4.7	18.6	100
Population	196,670,908	37,300,956	2,161,218	14,511,040	57,426,670	308,745,538

* *Native American* includes American Indians and Alaska Natives. *Asian* includes Asian Indians, Chinese, Filipino, Japanese, Korean, Vietnamese, other Asians, Native Hawaiians, and other Pacific Islanders. *Other* includes people of other single races and people of two or more races.

Note 1: The Hispanic category is not included here as it contains people from several racial categories. In addition, the US Census Bureau only started tracking Hispanic origin in the 1980 census. (See Section B of this activity.)

Note 2: Calculated population numbers may not exactly match Census Bureau statistics due to rounding.

Chapter 10 Marketing Research

Name _____

Section B

The US Census Bureau only started tracking Hispanic origin in the 1980 census. Tracking Hispanic origin is complicated because many Hispanic people claim a variety of racial origins, including White, Black, or more than one race. Therefore, population statistics for those of Hispanic origin are separate from the ethnic group statistics. In the chart that follows, calculate the missing percentages. 1980 is completed for you as an example.

Year	Hispanic Origin — White, Hispanic Origin	Hispanic, Origin of Any Race	Other Non Hispanic, Non White	Total
1980				
%	80	6	14	100
Population (Number)	180,256,366	14,608,673	31,680,766	226,545,805
1990				
%	76	9	15	100
Population (Number)	188,128,296	22,354,059	38,227,518	248,709,873
2000				
%	75	13	12	100
Population (Number)	211,460,626	35,305,818	34,655,462	281,421,906
2010				
%	64	16	20	100
Population (Number)	196,670,908	50,477,594	61,597,036	308,745,538

Part 3: Demonstrate Your Knowledge

Primary Data

Think of a store you know well, such as a clothing or book store, beauty salon, restaurant, or sporting goods store. The store's owners want to increase sales and customer satisfaction. Imagine you are the marketer hired to help them learn about their customers' needs and wants. You will use five methods to gather primary data. Complete the activity below.

Name of Store: _____

Location of Store: _____

Observation

1. You plan to visit the store as a secret shopper. List the top three goals for your secret-shopping session.
   Student answers will vary.

2. Describe what you would do during your secret-shopping session.
   Student answers will vary.

3. What information do you think you would be able to give the owners to help them increase both sales and customer satisfaction?
   Student answers will vary.

Interview

4. List two questions you could ask customers during an interview to learn what they think about the store and its products.
   Student answers will vary.

Survey

5. You are planning to do a brief customer survey. The survey questions will be accompanied by choices from which customers can quickly choose as answers. List two multiple choice questions with answer choices that you could include in your survey to get the information you need.
   Student answers will vary.

Chapter 10 Marketing Research

Name _____

6. What could you do to encourage customers to fill out the survey?
   Student answers will vary.

Diary

7. You plan to use a diary. What are the different types?
   Diaries can use an open- or forced-choice response format—or a combination of both.

8. Choose the type of diary you would use and give examples of two questions you would ask.
   Student answers will vary.

Experiment

9. You plan to do an experiment to gain customer information. State the hypothesis that you will use.
   Student answers will vary.

10. Describe your experiment.
    Student answers will vary.

Part 4: Be Your Own Leader

Setting Goals

As a leader, it is important to know how to set achievable goals. If you do not demand the best from yourself, how can you demand the best from others? To practice setting goals, complete the following activities in the space provided or on a separate sheet of paper.

1. Set a minimum of two SMART goals for yourself as a leader. Remember, SMART stands for specific, measurable, achievable, realistic, and timely. For example, each member of my CTSO will sell at least 40 green-bead necklaces in one week for $1.00 each to raise $600 for the Muscular Dystrophy Association (MDA) to send a child to camp. This is a SMART goal because it is:
   - Specific—specifies raising money for MDA and it includes all chapter members;
   - Measurable—the CTSO either reaches the $600 goal or does not;
   - Achievable—40 necklaces at $1.00 each is certainly doable for each person;
   - Realistic—a reasonable goal to achieve; and
   - Timely—one week to sell 600 necklaces.

SMART Goal #1

Student answers will vary.

SMART Goal #2

Student answers will vary.

2. Once your goals are set, identify the resources that you will need in order to achieve those goals. Fill in the following:

   People—list the people who can help you achieve each goal. Student answers will vary.

   Things—make a list of the things that you will need to achieve your goals.
   Student answers will vary.

   Money—will you need money to achieve your goal? If so, how much? How will you get the money?
   Student answers will vary.

3. In order to achieve each SMART goal, what specific actions will you need to take as the leader?

SMART Goal #1

Student answers will vary.

SMART Goal #2

Student answers will vary.

Name _____ Date _____ Period _____

CHAPTER 11
Competition

Part 1: Check Your Knowledge

Matching

Write the correct term for each definition on the line provided.

Key Terms

antitrust	market size
benefit	market structure
collusion	monopolistic competition
competitive advantage	monopoly
direct competitors	nonprice competition
feature	oligopoly
indirect competitors	perfect competition
market share	price competition
market-share leader	unique selling proposition (USP)

1. The statement summarizing the special features or benefits of a product or business.
   unique selling proposition (USP)

2. Company that sells products or services identical or very similar to the ones you sell.
   direct competitor

3. Fact about a product or service.
   feature

4. Term created by the government in an effort to fight the big corporate trusts that operated as monopolies.
   antitrust

5. A product or business offering better value, features, or service than the competition.
   competitive advantage

Copyright Goodheart-Willcox Co., Inc.   89

6. Offers different, but similar, products or services that could also meet customer needs.
   indirect competitors

7. How a market is organized based on the number of businesses competing for sales in an industry.
   market structure

8. A large number of small businesses selling similar, but not the same, products at different prices.
   monopolistic competition

9. A competitive advantage based on factors other than price.
   nonprice competition

10. Business leaders working together to remove their competition, set prices, and control distribution.
    collusion

11. A market structure with one business that has complete control of a market's entire supply of goods or services.
    monopoly

12. The percentage of the total sales that one business has in a specific market.
    market share

13. Companies with the largest combined market share.
    market-share leader

14. Characterized by a large number of small businesses selling the same products at the same prices.
    perfect competition

15. The total sales per year for a specific product.
    market size

Chapter 11   Competition

Name _____

True or False

Decide whether each statement is true or false and enter T or F on the line provided. If the statement is false, rewrite the statement to make it true.

1. Monopolies promote healthy competition.   False. Monopolies prevent healthy competition.

2. An oligopoly is a market structure with a small number of large companies selling the same or similar products.   True

3. Monopolistic competition is also known as imperfect competition.   True

4. Buying and selling with few government restrictions defines a market economy.   True

5. Competition is not a key element of both market and mixed economies.   False. Competition is a key element of both market and mixed economies.

6. In a command economy, the government acts as a monopoly.   True

7. The goal of antitrust laws is to make sure that markets are closed and noncompetitive.   False. The goal of antitrust laws is to make sure that markets remain open and competitive.

8. Price competition occurs when a higher price is the main reason for customers to buy from one business over another.   False. Price competition occurs when a lower price is the main reason for customers to buy from one business over another.

9. Benefits are the reasons a product will make the lives of customers easier or better.   True

10. One of the most efficient ways to evaluate a competitor's product is to buy it.   True

Copyright Goodheart-Willcox Co., Inc.

Part 2: Marketing by the Numbers

Market Share

The mobile phone industry is very competitive. The following chart shows the top-five mobile phone vendors, their unit shipments, and market shares for the second quarters of 2010 and 2011*. Complete the chart by computing the market share percent for each of the top-five mobile phone vendors during the second quarters of 2010 and 2011. In the last column, determine if the market share increased or decreased from 2010 to 2011. The first one has been done for you as an example.

Vendor	2011 2nd Quarter, Unit Shipments in Millions	2011 2nd Quarter Market Share	2010 2nd Quarter Unit Shipments in Millions	2010 2nd Quarter Market Share	Increase or Decrease from 2010 to 2011
1. Nokia	88.5	24.2%	111.1	33.8%	Decrease
2. Samsung	70.2	19.2%	63.8	19.4%	Increase
3. LG Electronics	24.8	6.8%	30.6	9.3%	Decrease
4. Apple	20.3	5.6%	8.4	2.6%	Increase
5. ZTE	16.6	4.5%	12.2	3.7%	Increase
6. Others	145	39.7%	102.3	31.2%	Increase
Total	365.4	100%	328.4	100%	

* IDC Worldwide Mobile Phone Tracker on July 28, 2011

Double-Bar Graphs

A double-bar graph is used to compare two kinds of information, using the same criteria. In this case, you will be comparing the unit shipments in millions for the six cell phone vendors during the second quarters of 2010 and 2011.

Provide a visual representation of the data in the chart using a double bar graph. The x-axis is the vendor and the y-axis is the unit shipment in millions. Use two bars per vendor to represent the data from 2010 and 2011.

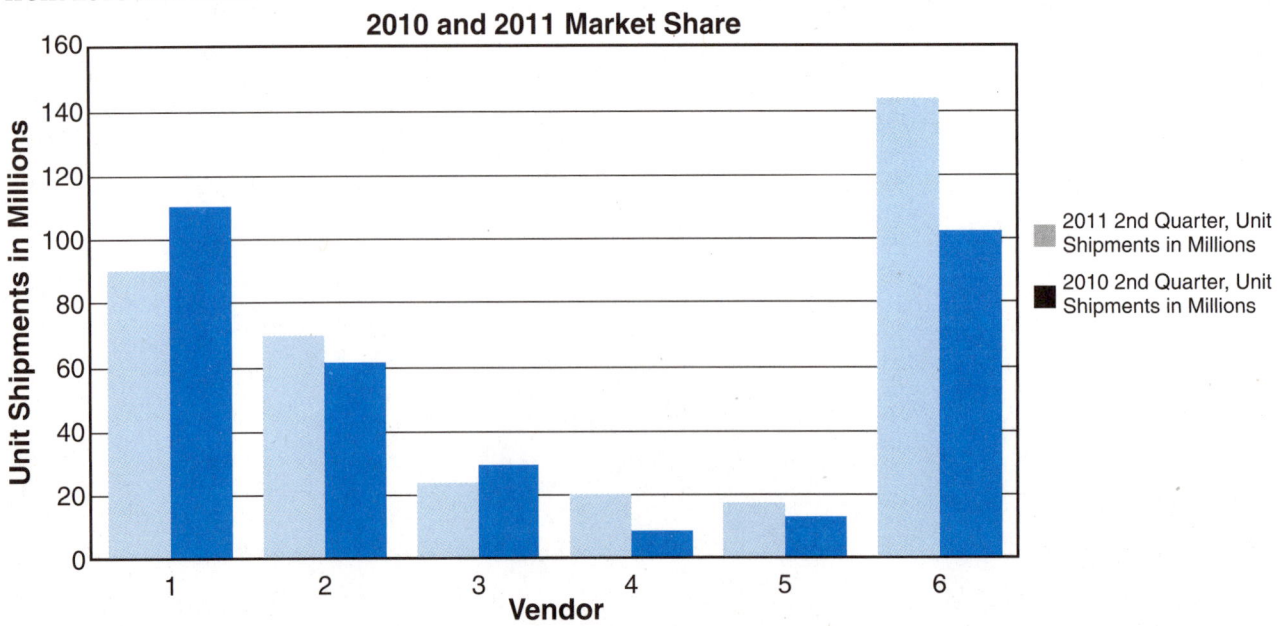

2010 and 2011 Market Share

[Double-bar graph showing Unit Shipments in Millions (y-axis, 0-160) by Vendor (x-axis, 1-6). Light blue bars represent 2011 2nd Quarter Unit Shipments; dark blue bars represent 2010 2nd Quarter Unit Shipments.]

Chapter 11 Competition

Name _____

Part 3: Demonstrate Your Knowledge

Marketing Needs

Imagine that you are a marketing specialist working with the entrepreneurs. Read each scenario that follows, then answer the questions with ideas that will help the entrepreneur get started.

A. Clothes for Grandma

Sue's grandmother lives in an assisted living center. Sue observes that her grandmother has a great deal of trouble with buttons and buttonholes, buckles, zippers, and ties. Many of the other residents have similar difficulties. Sue also observes that her grandmother could be more independent if she had clothing with easy closures. Sue sees a business opportunity. Sue has background in sewing and fashion design. She researches the field, and she learns that several companies produce clothing with Velcro fasteners. The clothing is cheap; however, the styles and colors are ugly.

1. What is the market need? *Clothing that is easy to put on, fasten, and unfasten.*

2. Who are the competitors? *Several producers*

3. What are the strengths and weaknesses of the competitors? *Strength: easy to put on; Weakness: clothing is unattractive*

4. What could the new (or modified) business have as its competitive edge? *Attractive styles and appealing colors*

5. On what basis could the new (or modified) business compete? *Nonprice—More fashion appeal would make wearers look and feel better, as well as making them feel more independent, so it might be worth it for them to pay more money*

B. Courier Service to the Suburbs

Derrick lives in a sprawling city. Businesses and professional offices in the downtown district often use a courier service to quickly transport documents and other important materials. The service is a "fleet" of two Mini Coopers. Demand for the courier service is so heavy downtown that the Minis do not pick up or deliver to the outer areas of the city or the surrounding suburbs. Derrick sees an opportunity, but is the market large enough for a courier service that focuses on the outer areas of the city and the suburbs?

1. What is the market need? *Courier service outside of the city center.*

2. Who are the competitors? *None in the area.*

3. What are the strengths and weaknesses of the competitors? *None in the area.*

Copyright Goodheart-Willcox Co., Inc.

93

4. What could the new (or modified) business have as its competitive edge? Provide service in an area where the service currently does not exist.

5. On what basis could the new (or modified) business compete? Nonprice— May have to charge more because the area served is larger and more spread out.

C. Specialties for S&S Diner

Steve and Sveta have a diner, the classy silver S&S. It is located near several large apartment complexes, mostly with retired, moderate-income residents. Nearby competitors include a family cafeteria and May's Tearoom. The S&S serves traditional diner foods—meatloaf, hamburgers, milkshakes, and mile-high pies. Business is okay, but Steve, an accomplished chef, is bored. Sveta is disappointed that their older neighbors do not eat there. Several have come in, read the menu, and left. Sveta thinks it might be because they are on special diets.

1. What is the market need?
Tasty restaurant meals that meet special dietary needs.

2. Who are the competitors?
Family cafeteria and May's Tearoom. Probably serve a variety of basic, plain foods.

3. What are the strengths and weaknesses of the competitors?
Probably serve a variety of basic, plain foods.

4. What could the new (or modified) business have as its competitive edge?
A classier setting, tasty meals to meet special needs created by Steve, a professional chef, and a desire to please an older market.

5. On what basis could the new (or modified) business compete?
Nonprice— Prices may need to be a little higher for the special meals, but the taste and convenience might be worth it to the older market.

Chapter 11   Competition

Name _____

Part 4: Be Your Own Leader

Leadership

If you do an online search of the word *leadership*, you will get about 460,000,000 hits. Why? Leadership is a topic that is constantly studied, researched, and written about. There are hundreds of books and thousands of articles on the topic. People in all walks of life want to be better leaders. Being a great leader takes practice, making mistakes, owning the mistakes, and trying again. One way to practice your leadership skills is by completing case studies that test your ability to make good decisions. Read the following case studies and think about what you would do as the leader in the organization. Answer the specific questions after each case.

1. The economy has taken a downturn. One year ago when you hired new staff for your marketing department, company sales were growing. Now, sales have decreased by almost 50%. You have three choices: lay off 10 people; reduce everyone's hours to 37 hours per week and institute a pay freeze; or require all employees to take a pay cut.

   a. Who will be included in making this decision? Why?

      Student answers will vary.
      _____
      _____

   b. When will you tell staff about the change—before or after you have made a final decision? Why?

      _____
      _____

   c. How will you get people to accept the change?

      _____
      _____

2. A client has contacted your graphic design firm and requested that you work on a new logo for their company. The client is planning to rebrand the company and will need the new logo in six weeks when the newly rebranded company is unveiled to the public. The logo will be used on all packaging, corporate communications, and marketing materials. If your firm cannot meet this deadline, the client will use a different graphic design firm for the job. Your staff is already maxed out and running behind on three other corporate accounts.

   a. How will you determine if this new assignment can be done?

      Student answers will vary.
      _____
      _____

   b. How will adding work to already overloaded staff affect their morale and motivation?

      _____
      _____

   c. What can you do to minimize the impact on staff morale and motivation?

      _____
      _____

Copyright Goodheart-Willcox Co., Inc.

3. Recently, the Fortune 500 company you work for has had a series of negative stories about it in the news. The stories include possible chemical leaks in local rivers, the closing of a plant and offshore production, and the firing of the CEO. As the marketing manager, you have been tasked with developing a community outreach program that will be implemented in any town or area in which one of your manufacturing plants is located. Your budget for the program is $5 million. You have six months to plan and implement the new program.

   a. Who will be included in the decision making? Why?

   Student answers will vary.

   b. How will you decide what to do? Why?

   c. How will you know when you have been successful?

Name _____ Date _____ Period _____

CHAPTER 12
Targeting a Market

Part 1: Check Your Knowledge

Matching

Write the correct term for each definition on the line provided.

Key Terms

attitude
behavioral segmentation
buying status
customer profile
demographic segmentation
discretionary income
disposable income
generation
geographic segmentation
market

mass market
mass marketing
niche market
psychographics
psychographic segmentation
target market
target marketing
usage rate
value

1. Divides a market by the relationships between customers and the product or service.
   behavioral segmentation

2. A piece of the target market that is very narrow and specific.
   niche market

3. A group of people born during a certain time in history.
   generation

4. What a person believes in.
   values

5. Describes when a customer will buy a product or service.
   buying status

Copyright Goodheart-Willcox Co., Inc. 97

6. Dividing the market of potential customers by their personal statistics.
   demographic segmentation

7. Segmenting a market based on where customers live.
   geographic segmentation

8. How often a customer buys or uses a product or service.
   usage rate

9. The specific group of customers at which a company aims its products and services.
   target market

10. Data about the preferences or choices of a group of people.
    psychographics

11. The remaining take-home pay after life necessities are paid for.
    discretionary income

12. How a person feels about something.
    attitude

13. Using unique marketing mixes for different target markets.
    target marketing

14. The overall market or group of people who might buy a product or service.
    mass market

15. The take-home pay a person has available to spend.
    disposable income

16. The people who might buy something.
    market

Chapter 12   Targeting a Market

Name _____

True or False

Decide whether each statement is true or false and enter *T* or *F* on the line provided. If the statement is false, rewrite the statement to make it true.

1. Markets are the focus of all marketing efforts. **True**

2. Correctly choosing the best target market is one of the most important decisions a marketer makes. **True**

3. Niche markets are often created by businesses looking for a market segment whose needs are already being met. **False. Niche markets are often created by businesses looking for a market segment whose needs are *not* being met.**

4. Mass marketing uses several marketing mixes of product, price, place, and promotion for a product. **False. Mass marketing uses one marketing mix of product, price, place, and promotion for a product.**

5. Mass marketing ignores customer differences. **True**

6. The term *product* includes goods and services but does *not* include ideas. **False. The term product includes goods, services, and ideas.**

7. Psychographic segmentation is dividing the market by certain preferences or lifestyle choices. **True**

8. Climate has a huge impact on what customers need. **True**

9. A customer profile is a general description of the competition in a market segment. **False. A customer profile is a detailed description of the typical consumer in a market segment.**

10. White collar generally refers to a job in which a person must wear work clothes or protective gear. **False. Blue collar generally refers to a job in which a person must wear work clothes or protective gear.**

Part 2: Marketing by the Numbers

Section A

In 2010, the US Census Bureau published the following demographic information, segmented by special age categories. Compute the percentage of the total population for each of these special segments of the population. Round the numbers to the nearest whole percent. Remember, some of the special age categories will overlap with each other. One of the categories has been completed for you as an example.

Demographic Segmentation by Special Age Categories

2010 Special Age Categories:	Total in Thousands	Percent	Males in Thousands	Percent	Females in Thousands	Percent
Total population	310,233	100%	152,753	50%	157,479	50%
5 to 13 years	37,123	12%	18,945	12%	18,178	12%
14 to 17 years	16,994	5%	8,713	6%	8,281	5%
18 to 24 years	30,713	10%	15,675	10%	15,037	10%
16 years and over	243,639	79%	118,739	78%	124,900	79%
18 years and over	235,016	76%	114,316	75%	120,700	77%
10 to 49 years	169,635	55%	85,727	56%	83,908	53%
16 to 64 years	203,410	66%	101,447	66%	101,963	65%
55 years and over	76,504	25%	34,766	23%	41,737	26%
65 years and over	40,229	13%	17,292	11%	22,937	15%
75 years and over	24,517	8%	9,247	6%	15,271	10%

Section B

Recall that double-bar graphs allow for the comparison of two kinds of information using the same criteria. In this case, you will be comparing the male and female counts (in the thousands) of special populations.

Provide a visual representation of the 2010 data in the chart by creating a double-bar graph using the following graph. The x-axis is the special age categories, and the y-axis is the population number in thousands. One bar will represent the female population and the other bar will represent the male population in each category.

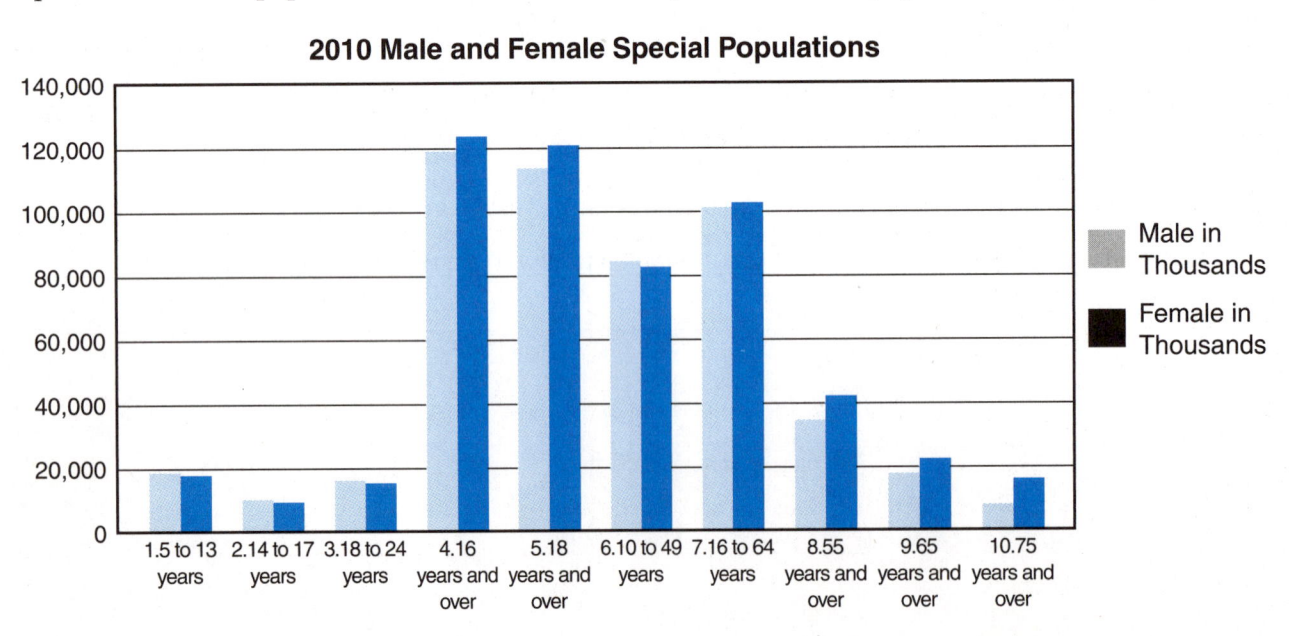

Chapter 12   Targeting a Market

Name _____

Part 3: Demonstrate Your Knowledge

Target Markets

Consider the following four qualities for a profitable target market:
1. Clearly defined wants and needs that your company can meet;
2. Money to buy your product;
3. Willingness and authority to buy your product; and
4. Enough customers in the market to be profitable.

Imagine you are the marketing manager for a company that produces premium-quality surround-sound systems. These systems are expensive and must be professionally installed in a home or business. Which of the following potential markets would be good targets for your surround-sound systems? Read each description, then write *yes* or *no* in the right column. In the space below each market, explain your reason for each answer.

Description of Market	Good Target?
1. Developers of condominiums for first-time buyers First-time buyers will usually not have the money for an expensive sound system, so the developer will not want to install it.	No
2. College students who share apartments or dorm rooms Most college students don't have the money for an expensive sound system. Also, most live in dorms or rented apartments, where they do not have the authority to install such a system.	No
3. Luxury resorts that want to promote their excellent amenities These resorts attract people willing to pay top dollar, so it is worthwhile for them to install the premium quality systems.	Yes
4. Public school music departments They cannot afford and do not need a premium system.	No
5. People who own or are building their own luxury homes These people are willing and able to pay for the system.	Yes
6. Convenience and bargain-store chains, such as Red Pantry and Dollar Tree Such stores do not need a premium system.	No
7. Independent retail music stores that cater to professional musicians The music store might want to offer a high-grade system for demonstrating instruments and speakers.	Possibly
8. A new high-end three-level mall under construction The owners may want to install a high-grade system for background music and announcements.	Yes
9. An indoor ice rink The owners may want a high-quality system for broadcasting play-by-play descriptions for hockey games or music for ice skating competitions.	Possibly
10. An outdoor professional sports stadium Not likely; it probably already has one installed.	No

Copyright Goodheart-Willcox Co., Inc.

Part 4: Be Your Own Leader

Creativity

Being a good leader often takes creativity and the ability to think outside the box. The following exercise may help you to improve your creativity and leadership skills.

1. Explain why creativity is important in leadership.
   Student answers will vary.

2. Identify a creative leader. What has he or she done that separates himself or herself from others?
   Student answers will vary.

3. Thinking outside of the box as a leader takes practice. Conduct an Internet search on *creative thinking*. What are five things you can do to think more creatively? List and explain each. Give an example for each.

Example 1
Student answers will vary.

Example 2

Example 3

Example 4

Example 5

Name _____ Date _____ Period _____

CHAPTER 13
Business-to-Consumer (B2C) Marketing

Part 1: Check Your Knowledge

Matching
Write the correct term for each definition on the line provided.

Key Terms

buying motive
consumer behavior
extensive decision-making process
hierarchy of needs
impulse buying decision
limited decision-making process
motivate
motive
peer pressure
psychological influence
reference group
routine buying decision
self-actualization
situational influence
social influence
value
word-of-mouth publicity

1. The actions taken by people to satisfy their needs and wants including what they buy.
   consumer behavior

2. An influence that comes from within a person or why a person has specific needs and wants.
   psychological influence

3. Some needs must be satisfied before others.
   hierarchy of needs

4. The need to express a person's true self through reaching personal goals and helping others.
   self-actualization

5. An internal push that causes a person to act.
   motive

6. To provide the internal push that results in action.
   motivate

Copyright Goodheart-Willcox Co., Inc. 103

7. The reason a consumer seeks and buys a product or service.
   buying motive

8. An influence from the society in which a person lives.
   social influence

9. A group of people who influence buying decisions.
   reference group

10. The social influence exerted on an individual by their peers.
    peer pressure

11. An influence that comes from the environment.
    situational influence

12. The relative worth of something.
    value

13. A purchase made quickly and with little thought.
    routine buying decision

14. Making a purchase that requires some amount of research and planning.
    limited decision-making process

15. Making a purchase that involves a great deal of research and planning.
    extensive decision-making process

Chapter 13   Business-to-Consumer (B2C) Marketing

Name _____

True or False

Decide whether each statement is true or false and enter *T* or *F* on the line provided. If the statement is false, rewrite the statement to make it true.

1. Not all needs are equal. True

2. According to Maslow, the strongest need is for safety. False. According to Maslow, the strongest needs are physical.

3. From a marketing viewpoint, the lower levels of Maslow's Hierarchy of Needs have the largest markets. True

4. Sometimes new products can create new needs or wants. True

5. Word-of-mouth publicity is advertising. False. Word-of-mouth publicity is the informal conversation people have about their experiences with a business and its products.

5. Good business owners and marketers make sure customers are satisfied with a purchase because it ensures repeat business. True

6. For consumers, value may be tied to price and brand. True

7. After a purchase, consumers never compare the recent purchase with earlier ones. False. After a purchase, consumers often compare the recent purchase with earlier ones.

8. A purchase made with planning or research is an impulse buying decision. False. An impulse buying decision is a purchase made with no planning or research.

9. Sometimes, expensive items are also purchased in a routine way. True

Copyright Goodheart-Willcox Co., Inc.

Part 2: Marketing by the Numbers

Estimating

Estimating is a useful skill both for consumers and marketers. Estimating can give you an idea of the total cost of several items when a calculator is not available. You can also use estimates to check calculations that you perform on a calculator. The estimate can let you know if your answer is close or where the decimal point should go. Estimating and rounding go hand in hand.

Estimating for Addition
1. Round each number to its largest place value.
2. Add the rounded numbers.

The following table shows two examples of estimating.

Example 1		Example 2	
Actual	Estimate	Actual	Estimate
3,465	3,000	23,456,790	20,000,000
2,891	3,000	67,922,563	70,000,000
6,782	7,000	81,103,528	80,000,000
1,935	2,000	77,834,652	80,000,000
8,324	8,000	34,291,298	30,000,000
Total	Total	Total	Total
23,397	23,000	284,608,831	280,000,000

How close are the estimates to the actual answers? To find the difference between the estimated actual totals, divide the difference between the two by the actual total. The result is the *percent of error*.

In the first example, the actual total of 23,397 minus the estimated total of 23,000 is 397. The difference of 397 is then divided by the actual total of 23,397. The answer is 0.016967987, which rounds to 0.017 or 1.7%. A 1.7 percent of error is fairly low. The percent of error in example 2 is 1.6%.

In these examples, the value of the estimates is that they let you know the place value of your answer. This information is useful when the answer is one or more place values higher than the numbers that were added, as in both examples.

For the following addition problems, first estimate each number to the highest place value and total the estimated numbers. Then, total the actual numbers and find the difference. Finally, calculate the percent of error for each problem.

Problem 1		Problem 2	
Actual	Estimate	Actual	Estimate
27	30	674	700
82	80	381	400
49	50	926	900
63	60	774	800
91	90	829	800
Total	Total	Total	Total
312	310	3,584	3,600
Difference: 2		Difference: 16	
Percent Error: 0.6%		Percent Error: 0.4%	

Chapter 13 Business-to-Consumer (B2C) Marketing

Name _____

| Problem 3 ||
Actual	Estimate
1,477	1,000
6,381	6,000
9,243	9,000
7,815	8,000
6,224	6,000
Total	Total
31,140	30,000
Difference: 1,140	
Percent Error: 3.7%	

| Problem 4 ||
Actual	Estimate
27,843	30,000
89,762	90,000
96,724	100,000
75,128	80,000
63,139	60,000
Total	Total
352,596	360,000
Difference: 7,404	
Percent Error: 2.1%	

| Problem 5 ||
Actual	Estimate
104,673	100,000
871,025	900,000
624,643	600,000
286,927	300,000
452,871	500,000
Total	Total
2,340,139	2,400,000
Difference: 59,861	
Percent Error: 2.6%	

| Problem 6 ||
Actual	Estimate
1,674,285	2,000,000
5,782,921	6,000,000
3,241,638	3,000,000
9,163,429	9,000,000
6,803,114	7,000,000
Total	Total
26,665,387	27,000,000
Difference: 334,613	
Percent Error: 1.3%	

| Problem 7 ||
Actual	Estimate
29,842,214	30,000,000
87,633,906	90,000,000
53,192,041	50,000,000
24,737,892	20,000,000
92,822,755	90,000,000
Total	Total
288,228,808	280,000,000
Difference: 8,228,808	
Percent Error: 2.9%	

| Problem 8 ||
Actual	Estimate
253,671,704	300,000,000
372,317,704	400,000,000
326,984,368	300,000,000
994,672,981	1,000,000,000
864,355,584	900,000,000
Total	Total
2,812,002,341	2,900,000,000
Difference: 87,997,659	
Percent Error: 3.1%	

Problem 9	
Actual	**Estimate**
4,453,974,624	4,000,000,000
8,906,837,697	9,000,000,000
7,631,504,465	8,000,000,000
4,972,753,812	5,000,000,000
3,148,613,537	3,000,000,000
Total	Total
29,113,684,135	29,000,000,000
Difference: 113,684,135	
Percent Error: 0.4%	

Problem 10	
Actual	**Estimate**
57,876,298,041,737	60,000,000,000,000
984,317,981,211	1,000,000,000,000
2,763,428,006	3,000,000,000
48,627,912	50,000,000
6,482,938,544	6,000,000,000
Total	Total
58,869,911,017,410	61,009,050,000,000
Difference: 2,139,138,982,590	
Percent Error: 3.6%	

Answer the following questions about the problems you completed.

1. How close were your estimates to your actual answers? Student answers will vary.

2. Describe when you might use estimating. Student answers will vary.

Chapter 13   Business-to-Consumer (B2C) Marketing

Name _____

Part 3: Demonstrate Your Knowledge

Section A

There are three levels of consumer buying decisions: routine, extensive, and limited. Read the following situations. In the spaces provided, write the type of buying decision that purchase will most likely involve. Also, explain your reasoning in detail using complete sentences.

Consumer
1. Every week, Mr. Lopez buys bread, juice, and cereal. He always chooses his family's favorite brands. 1) Routine; 2) Student answers will vary.
2. Damion has been using one of his dad's computers. However, it does not have all the features he wants. He has decided to shop for a new one. 1) Extensive; 2) Student answers will vary.
3. LaVonne has used her favorite brand of pen, the Pilot Razorpoint, for years. Recently, the pen has been discontinued. Therefore, LaVonne must find a replacement brand. 1) Limited; 2) Student answers will vary.

Section B

Promotional slogans often appeal directly to the needs identified in Maslow's Hierarchy. Review **Table 1** labeled *Sample Promotions*. Have you heard or seen advertisements using these promotional slogans? Are the company names or products familiar to you? If needed, discuss them with a partner. Then, on your own, complete the activity below.

Table 1

Sample Promotions	
Promotional Slogan	**Company and Product**
"A diamond is forever."	DeBeers diamonds
"A mind is a terrible thing to waste."	United Negro College Fund
"Advanced medicine for pain"	Advil headache medicine
"Built Ford tough"	Ford pick-up truck
"Connecting people"	Nokia cell phones
"Four doors never felt so secure."	Volvo automobile
"It's everywhere you want to be."	VISA credit card
"Just do it."	Nike athletic shoes
"Oh, what those oats can do!"	Quaker Oatmeal
"Take it for you. Take it for them."	Zyrtec allergy medicine
"Thirst quencher"	Gatorade drink
"This is no place for germs."	Lysol cleaner
"Unlike any other "	Mercedes-Benz automobile
"When you care enough to send the very best"	Hallmark greeting cards
"You're in good hands with Allstate."	Allstate Insurance

1. In your opinion, which slogan has had the most success? Explain why.
   Student answers will vary.

2. Which slogan appeals to you the most? The least? Explain your answers.
   Student answers will vary.

(Continued on next page.)

Chapter 13 Business-to-Consumer (B2C) Marketing

Name _____

Table 2 below lists each of the five needs. For each situation/state, write the promotional slogan from Table 1 that addresses the related need. The first one has been done for you.

Table 2

Promotions and Maslow's Needs	
Situation/State	Promotional Slogan
PHYSICAL	
Headache pain	"Advanced medicine for pain," Advil
Heart health	"Oh, what those oats can do!" Quaker
Thirst	"Thirst quencher," Gatorade
SAFETY	
From accidents	"Four doors never felt so secure," Volvo
From financial disaster	"You're in good hands with Allstate"
From germs and disease	"This is no place for germs!" Lysol
ACCEPTANCE	
Affection	"A diamond is forever," DeBeers
Belonging	"Connecting people," Nokia
Fitting in	"Take it for you. Take it for them." Zyrtec
ESTEEM	
Prestige	"Unlike any other," Mercedes-Benz
Quality	"When you care enough to send the very best," Hallmark
Self-image	"Built Ford tough," Ford
SELF-ACTUALIZATION	
Adventure	"It's everywhere you want to be," VISA
Aspirations	"Just do it," Nike
Knowledge	"A mind is a terrible thing to waste," United Negro College Fund

Copyright Goodheart-Willcox Co., Inc.

Part 4: Be Your Own Leader

Top Business Leaders—Will You Be Next?

Read about the following business leaders. Choose one of the leaders to conduct research on that leader. Learn more about his or her background, style of leadership, and reasons for success. Answer the questions about your chosen leader.

Zhang Xin, CEO of SOHO China

As of 2012, SOHO China the largest commercial real estate developer in Beijing. Born to educated parents that were sent to be "reeducated" in rural China, Zhang Xin grew up poor. So poor, in fact, that at one time she slept on her mother's desk with a dictionary as her pillow. As a teen, she worked 12-hour days in a sweatshop. However, once she had saved enough money, she bought a one-way ticket to London. That is where her business story begins. Xin learned the English language and a master's degree in economic development and went to work for Goldman Sachs on Wall Street. By 1994, however, she wanted to return home because the Chinese economy was changing. Xin met her husband in China and together they built SOHO China, which is worth over $10 billion.

Anne Mulcahy, CEO of Xerox

Mulcahy was selected to be the CEO in the midst of the company's financial crisis that could have forced Xerox into bankruptcy. She refused to put the company into bankruptcy and began to take bold moves to change the company. She reduced the workforce, flew across the country meeting with current and former customers, and eventually turned the company back into a profitable global leader. Mulcahy not only turned the company around, she reinvented it. Her advice is, "Focus on client service instead of financial engineering."

Howard Schultz, President and CEO of Starbucks

Courage, vision, and hard work helped a poor kid from the Bronx rise to such a high level of success. Howard Schultz worked hard to get a job at Starbucks after visiting the original Pikes Peak store in Seattle. After being rejected as the new marketing manager, Schultz called back the next day to lay out his reasoning why he was the best person for the job and he was given the position. Eventually, Schultz would leave Starbucks, start his own company, and then purchase Starbucks from the original owners. His vision led to Starbucks becoming a global chain with stand-alone stores, kiosks in stores and malls, and a worldwide, easily recognizable name.

Jeff Bezos, Founder and CEO of Amazon

Ever made a purchase at Amazon and then gone back to shop on the site again? If you have, you may remember that the website recommends products to you. How does it know what you might want? It uses a program to monitor your search history and your buying habits and then finds products that match them. Called *predictive analytics*, Bezos used the concept to revolutionize online shopping, making Amazon one of the fastest-growing Internet companies in the world.

1. Which leader did you research?

   Student answers will vary.

2. Describe the leader's background before joining or starting the company.

   Student answers will vary.

3. What is the person's leadership style?
   Student answers will vary.

4. What do you see as his or her greatest leadership trait(s)?
   Student answers will vary.

5. What did you learn about leadership from your research?
   Student answers will vary.

Name _____ Date _____ Period _____

CHAPTER 14: Business-to-Business (B2B) Marketing

Part 1: Check Your Knowledge

Matching

Write the correct term for each definition on the line provided.

Key Terms

bid
business purchasing
buyer
external influence
government market
institution
internal influence
inventory
NAICS
organizational buyer
producer
purchasing agent
reseller
service business
situational influence
supplier

1. A numerical system used to classify businesses and collect economic statistics.
   NAICS

2. The activity of acquiring goods or services to accomplish the goals of an organization.
   business purchasing

3. A formal written proposal that lists all of the goods and services that will be provided by a supplier, their prices, and timeline.
   bid

4. Includes national, state, and local government offices and agencies that buy a wide variety of products and services.
   government market

5. In companies with purchasing departments, the title of people who buy goods and services the company needs internally to operate its business.
   purchasing agent

Copyright Goodheart-Willcox Co., Inc.

6. A buying influence from outside the company that may include business competition, new technology, or product trends.
   external influence

7. Provide services to consumers or other businesses.
   service business

8. The person who buys products for a business.
   organizational buyer

9. Business that buys finished products to resell them to consumers.
   reseller

10. Includes public and private nonprofit organizations.
    institution

11. The goods a business has on hand to sell to customers.
    inventory

12. Buys raw materials and equipment that are used to make products and product components.
    producer

13. A buying influence from the environment in which the business exists that can include the economy, political environment, and regulations or laws.
    situational influence

14. The person responsible for planning and ordering inventory.
    buyer

15. Influences that come from within the business itself including the structure, goals, and management team of a company.
    internal influence

Chapter 14 Business-to-Business (B2B) Marketing

117

Name _____

True or False

Decide whether each statement is true or false and enter T or F on the line provided. If the statement is false, rewrite the statement to make it true.

1. Targeting business-market segments is always different than targeting consumer-market segments. False. In some ways, targeting business-market segments is similar to targeting consumer-market segments.

2. Business customers use the products they buy to make new products, resell to customers, or to operate the business. True

3. Business customers have exactly the same buying needs and motives as consumers. False. Business customers have very different buying needs and motives than consumers.

4. A B2B sale may take a long time to close and is based on relationship selling. True

5. There is generally no impulse buying in the business market. True

6. A modified purchase is a decision to buy a new product requiring a great deal of research and thought. False. A new purchase is a decision to buy a new product requiring a great deal of research and thought.

7. The word *organization* is another term for business. True

8. A business that sells to organizational buyers is called a *vendor*. True

9. Purchasing agents often need technical knowledge about their company's products or production processes. True

10. Due to the amount of money invested in business purchases, an informal or verbal bidding process is often used. False. Due to amount of money invested in business purchases, a formal bidding process is often used.

Part 2: Marketing by the Numbers

Calculating Charges

As you learned in this chapter, every business needs goods and services to run effectively. Most businesses need various office supplies to operate. Calculating charges is an important part of ordering, and accuracy is important. Calculating charges involves the following steps:

1. Find the correct price for the item.
2. Multiply by the number of items ordered.
3. Apply discounts or coupons.
4. Add any additional charges for delivery or installation.
5. Add proper taxes.

The following items appear in an office supply catalog:

Item	Price
Standard white business envelopes, 500 per box	$ 8.76
Self-sealing single window business envelopes, 500 per box	$ 19.22
Manila clasp envelopes, 9"x12", 100 per box	$ 13.52
Manila clasp envelopes, 10"x13", 100 per box	$ 16.17
First Class white wove envelopes, 10"x13", 100 per box	$ 19.36
ADDITIONAL CHARGES and DISCOUNTS: 15% Discount on orders of $150 or more $20 Delivery charge 5% Sales tax	

Calculate the charges for the following purchase orders.

Purchase Order 1			
Item	Price	Quantity	Total
White business envelopes	$8.76/500	2,000	35.04
Manila clasp envelopes, 9"x12"	$13.52/100	1,000	135.20
		Subtotal	170.24
		Less discount	25.54
		Merchandise total	144.70
		Sales tax	7.24
		Shipping charges	20.00
		Total charges	$ 171.94

Chapter 14   Business-to-Business (B2B) Marketing

Name _____

Purchase Order 2			
Item	Price	Quantity	Total
Self-sealing single window business envelopes	$19.22/500	1,500	57.66
Manila clasp envelopes, 9"x12"	$13.52/100	500	67.60
Manila clasp envelopes, 10"x13"	$16.17/100	500	80.85
First Class white wove envelopes, 10"x13"	$19.36/100	500	96.80
		Subtotal	302.91
		Less discount	45.44
		Merchandise total	257.47
		Sales tax	12.87
		Shipping charges	20.00
		Total charges	$ 290.34

Purchase Order 3			
Item	Price	Quantity	Total
White business envelopes	$8.76/500	3,500	61.32
Self-sealing single window business envelopes	$19.22/500	4,500	172.98
Manila clasp envelopes, 9"x12"	$13.52/100	2,700	365.04
First Class white wove envelopes, 10"x13"	$19.36/100	1,200	232.32
		Subtotal	831.66
		Less discount	124.75
		Merchandise total	706.91
		Sales tax	35.35
		Shipping charges	20.00
		Total charges	$ 762.26

Copyright Goodheart-Willcox Co., Inc.

Part 3: Demonstrate Your Knowledge

Business Buying Influences

Influences on business buying decisions include internal, external, and situational. Recall that influences on consumers include psychological, social, and situational. Read the following scenarios and determine the influences on the decisions.

The president of a printing firm has decided the company should purchase a costly new press that can also be programmed to make fancy folds, such as alternating, diagonal, and accordion. Last year, the company had only two orders for fancy folds. However, the president does not want to turn away business or outsource any order. Now the purchaser must get bids on the new press.

1. Which type of influence has affected this business decision? *internal*
2. What is the similar influence on consumer decisions? *psychological*

A natural disaster, such as an earthquake or hurricane, can lead to expansion for some businesses. Companies dealing with cleaning, construction, insurance, landscaping, and general household goods can do very well when there is an increased need for their products. A disaster clean-up company decides to expand following a violent hurricane season.

3. Which type of influence has affected this business decision? *situational*
4. What is the influence on a consumer's decision to use these services after a storm? *situational*

Travel on Two is a manufacturer of stand-up scooters, bicycles, and mopeds. The company's marketers have noticed a revival in popularity of the Vespa, a comfortable Italian motor scooter. The marketers urged the company to launch its own version of this vintage vehicle. The company decides to do so.

5. Which type of influence has affected this business decision? *external*
6. What is the similar influence on consumer decisions? *social*

Chapter 14 Business-to-Business (B2B) Marketing

Name _____

Part 4: Be Your Own Leader

Learning the Language

The following are a series of leadership terms and their definitions. Match the term to the correct definition. Before you can do that, however, you may have to conduct an Internet search to find the meanings of many of the terms. Once you have correctly matched the terms with their definitions, create your own set of flash cards to help you remember the terms. Write a term on one side of the card and the definition on the other side.

Leadership Terms

1. __m__ situational leadership
2. __h__ vision
3. __i__ vision Statement
4. __d__ servant Leader
5. __f__ authoritarian Leader
6. __l__ theories of leadership
7. __g__ mentor
8. __j__ trait theories of leadership
9. __o__ leadership
10. __k__ transformational leaders
11. __b__ delegating
12. __n__ coaching
13. __c__ directing
14. __a__ laissez-faire leadership
15. __e__ democratic leadership

Definitions

a. Leader gives all authority to followers; takes a hands-off approach to leading.
b. Giving responsibility for making a decision to another person
c. Leader tells other people exactly what to do.
d. Leader puts the organization's needs before him or herself.
e. Leader asks for the input of others before making decisions.
f. Leader makes all of the decisions.
g. An advisor, a counselor, a guide.
h. A long term strategy for reaching goals.
i. A statement that guides an organization.
j. Theories that believe specific traits, such as character, personality, etc., separate leaders from followers.
k. Leaders who have a profound effect on others.
l. Beliefs and/or ideas about what makes a true leader.
m. Leader changes leadership style based on what is occurring.
n. To train or instruct others to become better leaders.
o. Process of influencing others to achieve goals.

Copyright Goodheart-Willcox Co., Inc.

Name _____ Date _____ Period _____

CHAPTER 15
Products and Services

Part 1: Check Your Knowledge

Matching
Write the correct term for each definition on the line provided.

Key Terms

business product
category manager
consumer product
convenience good
decline stage
direction
feature
growth stage
guarantee
inseparability
installation
intangible
introduction stage
maturity stage
option
packaging
perishability
product depth
product item
product life cycle
product line
product manager
product mix
product planning
product/service management
product width
quality
saturated market
shopping good
specialty good
usage
variability
warranty

1. The time when a new product is first brought to the market.
   introduction stage

2. A marketing professional who guides the selection of products and oversees the marketing and sales of those products.
   product manager

3. The process of deciding which product elements to include that will appeal to the target market.
   product planning

Copyright Goodheart-Willcox Co., Inc. 123

4. A written document stating the quality of a product and promising to correct specific problems that might occur.
   warranty

5. The way something is used.
   usage

6. A feature that can be added to a product by customer request.
   option

7. Performs the same functions as a product manager but is responsible for an entire category of products.
   category manager

8. An item sold to businesses to keep them operating, as in B2B.
   business product

9. A product sold to consumers for their personal use, as in B2C.
   consumer product

10. All of the products and services a business sells.
    product mix

11. Something that cannot be touched, tried out before purchase, or returned.
    intangible

12. One of the steps that must be carried out in a specific order to complete a task successfully.
    direction

13. A fact about a product or service.
    feature

14. The creation of the service cannot be separated from its use.
    inseparability

15. Each service is nearly always unique.
    variability

16. The degree of a product's excellence.
    quality

17. The act or process of making a good ready for use in a certain place.
    installation

18. Protects products until customers are ready to use them.
    packaging

Chapter 15   Products and Services

Name _____

19. A promise that a product has a certain quality or will perform in a specific way.
    guarantee

20. Because services are intangible, they cannot be stored for later use.
    perishability

21. The group of closely related products within the product mix.
    product line

22. A good that is usually bought often with little effort and for immediate use.
    convenience good

23. The organizational structure that manages the development, marketing, and sale of a product or products.
    product/service management

24. The period in which product sales increase rapidly.
    growth stage

25. A unique item that consumers are willing to spend considerable time, effort, and money to buy.
    specialty good

26. The specific model, color, or size of a product in a line.
    product item

27. A good usually purchased after making the effort to compare price, quality, and style in more than one store.
    shopping good

28. The stages a product or a product category goes through from its beginning to end.
    product life cycle

29. When product sales begin to decrease.
    decline stage

30. The number of product lines a company offers.
    product width

True or False

Decide whether each statement is true or false and enter *T* or *F* on the line provided. If the statement is false, rewrite the statement to make it true.

1. If you do not have a product to sell, you do not need the other elements of the marketing mix.
   True

2. Many products are combinations of both goods and services. True

3. Premium-quality products rarely have the highest prices. False. Premium-quality products usually have the highest prices.

4. Moderate quality is an adequate level of product quality. False. Value quality is an adequate level of product quality.

5. Marketers often promote product safety features because such features can influence buying decisions.
   True

6. When marketers develop a product that requires maintenance and repair services, they must also plan for those services. True

7. The product depth is the number of product lines a company offers. False. The product depth is the number of product items within a product line.

8. Component parts are used in product manufacturing, but are not identifiable. False. Process materials are used in product manufacturing, but are not identifiable.

9. The maturity stage occurs when product sales are stable. True

10. A saturated market is one in which most of the potential customers who need, want, and can afford a product have *not* bought it. False. A saturated market is one in which most of the potential customers who need, want, and can afford a product have already bought it.

Part 2: Marketing by the Numbers

Product Life Cycle

Best Brands, Inc., has hired you as a marketing consultant to analyze the product life cycle of two of its recently introduced products. Use the data provided to make a product life cycle graph for each product. On each graph, label the four stages: introduction, growth, maturity, and decline. As the marketing consultant for each of these products, predict the future sales.

Time (in months)	Product A Sales (in dollars)	Product B Sales (in dollars)
0	0	0
6	$5,000	$10,000
12	5,000	20,000
18	10,000	40,000
24	15,000	40,000
30	20,000	40,000
36	30,000	40,000
42	40,000	30,000
48	50,000	25,000
54	40,000	20,000

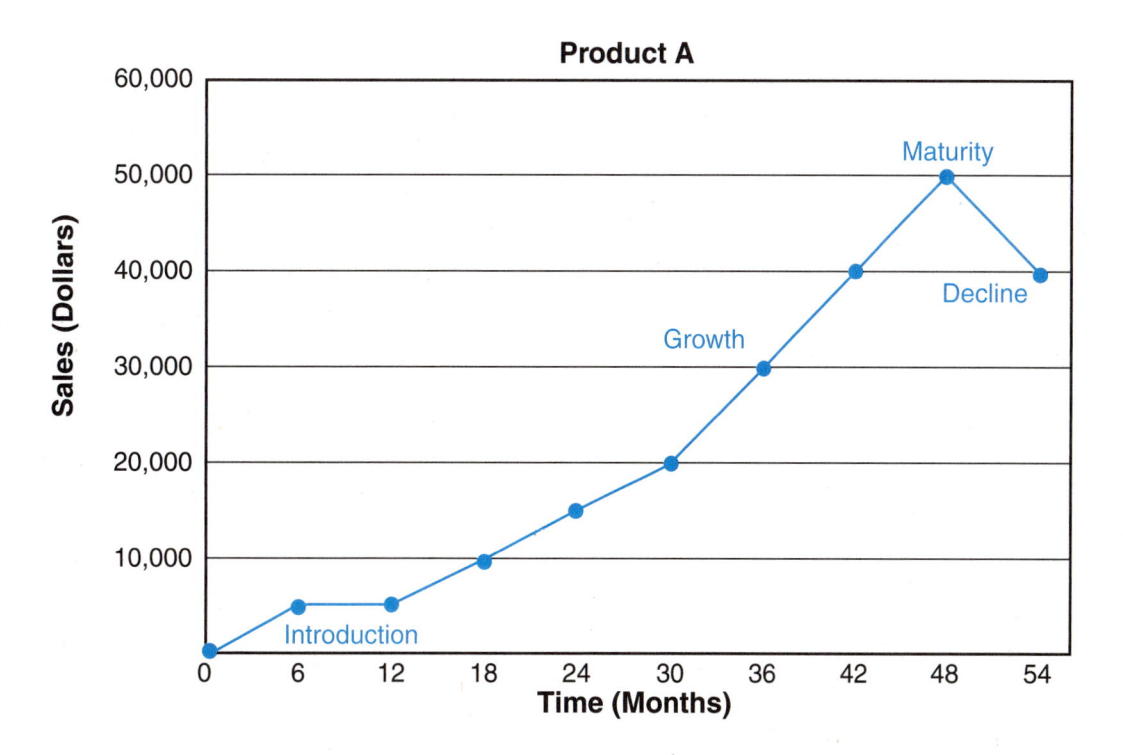

Product A

(Graph showing sales over time with stages labeled: Introduction, Growth, Maturity, Decline)

1. Plot the graph, label the introduction, growth, maturity, and decline stages for Product A.
2. What is your prediction for future sales?
   Student answers will vary.

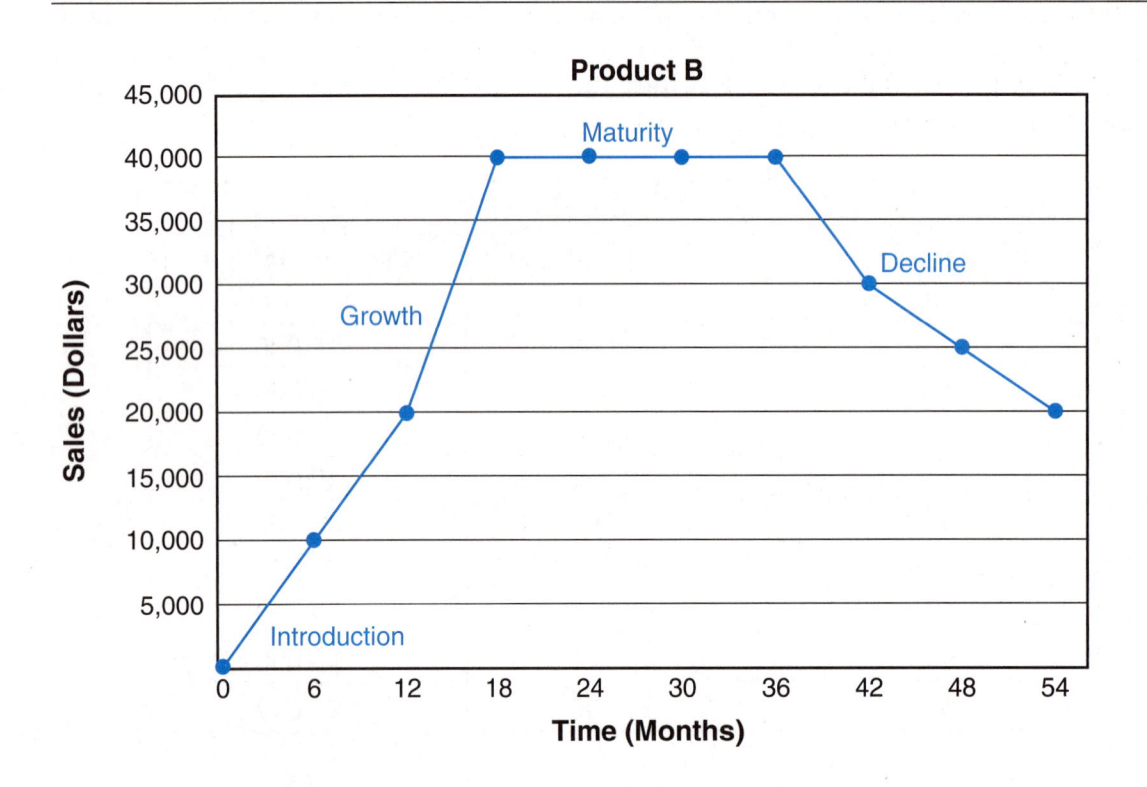

Product B

Graph: Sales (Dollars) vs. Time (Months)
- Introduction: (0, 0), (6, 10,000)
- Growth: (12, 20,000)
- Maturity: (18, 40,000), (24, 40,000), (30, 40,000), (36, 40,000)
- Decline: (42, 30,000), (48, 25,000), (54, 20,000)

1. Plot the graph, label the introduction, growth, maturity, and decline stages for Product B.
2. What is your prediction for future sales?
   Student answers will vary.

Chapter 15   Products and Services

129

Name _____

Part 3: Demonstrate Your Knowledge

Section A

The experience of attending a sporting event involves the purchase and use of many products—by both the business and the consumers. Below is a list of products or product categories. After each product or category, list all of the terms that apply: *good, service, idea, tangible, intangible, inseparable, variable, perishable, consumer product, business product.*

1. Tickets to the game
    service, intangible, inseparable, variable, perishable, consumer product

2. Caps, pennants, T-shirts, and other souvenirs
    good, tangible, consumer product

3. Arena expenses (light, sanitation, maintenance, security)
    service, intangible, inseparable, variable, perishable, business product

4. Food
    good, service, tangible, intangible, inseparable, perishable, consumer product

5. Intermission entertainment
    service, intangible, inseparable, variable, perishable, consumer product

6. Parking and shuttle bus service
    service, intangible, inseparable, variable, perishable, consumer product

Section B

Imagine you are a marketing consultant for a company that is creating a new product. Answer the questions for each of the three products.

1. Dinner-dance fundraising event to benefit art education.

    a. Is your product a good, service, or idea?
    combination of idea, service, and good

    b. Your product can come in three quality levels: value, moderate, and premium. Describe them in terms of features and options.
    Student answers will vary.

    c. Describe three possible target markets and the quality level that would be best for each.
    Student answers will vary.

Copyright Goodheart-Willcox Co., Inc.

2. High-end refrigerators

   a. Is your product a good, service, or idea?

   good

   b. Your product can come in three quality levels: value, moderate, and premium. Describe them in terms of features and options.

   Student answers will vary.

   c. Describe three possible target markets and the quality level that would be best for each.

   Student answers will vary.

3. Remodeling homes to make them handicapped accessible

   a. Is your product a good, service, or idea?

   Combination service and good

   b. Your product can come in three quality levels: value, moderate, and premium. Describe them in terms of features and options.

   Student answers will vary.

   c. Describe three possible target markets and the quality level that would be best for each.

   Student answers will vary.

Chapter 15   Products and Services

Name _____

Part 4: Be Your Own Leader

Learning from Leaders

After reading the following case study about the well-known leader, Nelson Mandela, answer the questions using complete sentences.

Nelson Mandela: Former President of South Africa

What does an influential political figure have to do with marketing? Everything. Marketing means influencing others by helping others to see the value of your viewpoint and promoting your ideas so others will join your cause. Nelson Mandela was both a prisoner and president, and he understood how to lead, regardless of where he found himself. Mandela is credited with being the person who was responsible for ending *apartheid*, or severe racial inequality, in his country in 1994. He was then elected the first black president of South Africa. In an interview conducted after retiring as president, Mandela shared some of the lessons he had learned as a leader.

Courage is not showing your fear.

Mandela once flew on a plane that had lost an engine approximately twenty minutes before landing. People on the plane began to panic until they noticed Mandela calmly reading his newspaper. When the plane landed, he told the person meeting him that he was "terrified up there." Mandela was often afraid, but he learned that by appearing fearless, he could inspire others.

Inspire others to join you.

When Mandela began to negotiate with the apartheid government of South Africa, which he had been fighting against for so long, people thought he had lost courage. However, Mandela took the time to explain to his followers why he was negotiating, what he was negotiating for, and where he would (and would not) compromise to reach their goal of freedom. His followers trusted him and continued to provide their support. Mandela was thinking in years, not days or weeks. He knew that over time, people would come to see that apartheid was wrong.

Appearance matters.

Even when Mandela was a law student, he had one thread-bare suit that he wore whenever it was necessary. He also understood the power of a smile. His smile would light up a room and disarm even those who stood against him. Once he became president of South Africa, he wore shirts made of bright and fun materials, signaling his joy as a leader and his positive outlook.

Keep your friends close and your enemies even closer.

Whether during the 27 years he spent in prison for his beliefs or the five years he spent as the president of his country, Mandela knew it was important to include others, especially if they held opposing views. He chose to keep those he did not fully trust as close to him as possible by including them in his cabinet. In this way, he always knew what they were doing, and he could influence them for the good of the country.

Copyright Goodheart-Willcox Co., Inc.

1. For each of Mandela's leadership lessons, write an example of a time when you experienced something similar or how you would follow his example.

   a. Courage is not showing your fear.

   Student answers will vary.

   b. Inspire others to join you.

   Student answers will vary.

   c. Appearance matters.

   Student answers will vary.

   d. Keep your friends close and your enemies even closer.

   Student answers will vary.

2. Add two of your own lessons in leadership to the four provided and give an example for each. Explain why these are important lessons for leaders.

   a. Leadership Lesson 1: Title _____

   b. Example

   Student answers will vary.

   c. Why it is important?

   Student answers will vary.

   a. Leadership Lesson 2: Title _____

   b. Example

   Student answers will vary.

   c. Why it is important?

   Student answers will vary.

Name _____ Date _____ Period _____

CHAPTER 16
New Product Development

Part 1: Check Your Knowledge

Matching

Write the correct term for each definition on the line provided.

Key Terms

brand
commercialization
creativity
image
new product
prototype
release date
repackaging
repositioning
reverse engineering
test marketing
trade show
trial run
virtual test market

1. A computer simulation of consumers, companies, and market environments.
   virtual test market

2. The date a new product is available for sale.
   release date

3. The ability to make new things or think of new ideas.
   creativity

4. A product that is different in some way from existing products.
   new product

Copyright Goodheart-Willcox Co., Inc.   133

5. Consists of testing the service on a few select customers to make sure that everything runs smoothly.
   trial run

6. The idea that people have about someone or something.
   image

7. Using new packaging on the same product; another common way to create a new product.
   repackaging

8. A large gathering of businesses for the purpose of displaying products for sale.
   trade show

9. A name, term, or design that sets a product or business apart from its competition.
   brand

10. Marketing an existing product in a new way to create a new position in the minds of customers to increase sales.
    repositioning

Chapter 16 New Product Development   **135**

Name _____

True or False

Decide whether each statement is true or false and enter *T* or *F* on the line provided. If the statement is false, rewrite the statement to make it true.

1. Often, a small change to an existing product is considered to be a new product. True

2. New products replace those at the beginning of their life cycles. False. New products replace those at the end of their life cycles.

3. The cost and risk of developing products or technology is small. False. The cost and risk of developing products or technology is great.

4. Many existing products can end up being valuable for other uses than the original one. True

5. One of the main reasons for a failed product is the lack of planning and research. True

6. Marketing research is *not* critical to planning and developing new products to meet customer needs and wants. False. Marketing research is critical to planning and developing new products to meet customer needs and wants.

7. A prototype is a working model of a new product for testing purposes. True

8. Test marketing introduces a new product to a small portion of the target market, one city for example, to learn how it will sell. True

9. Reverse engineering is assembling an object—usually in order to produce something similar. False. Reverse engineering is taking apart an object to see how it was made—usually in order to produce something similar.

10. Commercialization is the growth stage of the product life cycle. False. Commercialization is the introduction stage of the product life cycle.

Copyright Goodheart-Willcox Co., Inc.

Part 2: Marketing by the Numbers

Production Costs

The costs of producing goods can be divided into supplies and equipment. Manufacturers need to keep track of total costs and costs per item. Information for costs at a jeans factory follows. Calculate the costs and fill in the chart. Then, answer the questions.

Supplies				
Materials Needed per Pair of Jeans	Cost ($)	Quantity per Pair	Cost for 5,000 pairs ($)
2 Yards of Denim Material	$1.12/yard	2	$ 11,200.00
Industrial Sized Spool of Thread	$1.63	1	$ 8,150.00
Zipper	$1.55	1	$ 7,750.00
Metal button	$0.60	1	$ 3,000.00
Total Cost of Materials Needed			$ 30,100.00

Equipment			
Type of Equipment	Cost Each ($)	Quantity	Total Cost ($)
Industrial Sewing Machine	$ 650.00	10	$ 6,500.00
Material Cutter	$ 2,095.00	1	$ 2,095.00
Cutting Shears	$ 36.95	10	$ 369.50
Total Cost of Materials Needed			$ 8,964.50

1. What is the cost for equipment per pair of jeans when producing 5,000 pairs of jeans produced?
   $1.79 [$8,964.50/5,000 = $1.7929]

2. What is the total cost of equipment and supplies when producing 5,000 pairs of jeans produced?
   $39,064.50

3. What is the cost for materials and equipment per pair of jeans produced?
   $7.81 [$39,064.50/5,000 = $7.8129]

4. If there were an additional order for 5,000 more jeans, would the cost for materials per pair of jeans produced increase, decrease, or stay the same? Why? Stay the same if no quantity discount.

5. If there were an additional order for 5,000 more jeans, would the cost for equipment per pair of jeans produced increase, decrease, or stay the same? Why? Decrease; the equipment was already purchased.

Chapter 16 New Product Development   137

Name _____

Part 3: Demonstrate Your Knowledge

Section A

Read the following example of how a new product idea was developed. Then answer the question.

Tamara Monosoff walked into her bathroom to find that her toddler had unrolled a full roll of toilet paper from its holder. She imagined that an elastic strap fastened across the paper—something like an old-fashioned hair curler—would keep a mess like this from happening again. Aha! A new product idea. She found an engineer to draw the design, a machinist to make a prototype, a lawyer to register her patent, and a manufacturing plant to turn out the first batch. Within a year, the TP Saver was on the market and making money. The TP Saver is just one example of the thousands of baby products being sold today. With Americans spending six billion dollars a year on their babies, it is a great field for new products.

1. What method(s) did Tamara use to come up with her new product idea? _observation and creative thinking_

Section B

Now you will come up with your own product idea. Follow these steps.

1. **Choose a field.** Circle one of these fields or come up with one of your own.

    housecleaning   grocery shopping
    keeping organized   hair care and styling
    pet care   yard work
    baby and child care   car upkeep and accessories

    Your own idea for a field for your new product: _Student answers will vary._

2. **Change your viewpoint.** Look at the field through someone else's eyes. For example, imagine that you are a cat or dog. What does your human *not* understand? Write your suggestion for how to change your viewpoint for the field you chose. _Student answers will vary._

3. **List the problem.** Identify the problem to be solved or the need to be met. _Student answers will vary._

4. **Set your mind free.** Brainstorm 10 new product ideas. Let your senses help. What weight, size, color, material, or sound is appealing? Do not worry about how good the ideas are or whether they will work. _Student answers will vary._

5. **Screen your ideas.** Choose the one best idea. Describe the idea. Explain why it might sell. Describe the target market. _Student answers will vary._

Copyright Goodheart-Willcox Co., Inc.

Part 4: Be Your Own Leader

Lead From the Beginning

There are many great business leaders. Before beginning this exercise brainstorm five business leaders that you admire. You may need to do some research if you are not able to think of five business leaders.

Business leaders I admire:
Student answers will vary.

Choose one of the business leaders you listed above. As you conduct your research, answer the following questions and identify four important leadership traits he or she possesses. Write the leadership traits on the Leadership Graphic Organizer. Be prepared to present the information to the class.

1. What does this person do that makes him or her a leader?
   Student answers will vary.

2. What style of leadership does this person utilize?
   Student answers will vary.

3. Describe the impact the person has had on others as a leader.
   Student answers will vary.

4. What are the four traits you most admire about this leader? For each trait, provide an example.
   Student answers will vary.

Graphic Organizer

Place the name of the leader in the middle circle with the four leadership traits in the surrounding circles.

Student answers will vary.

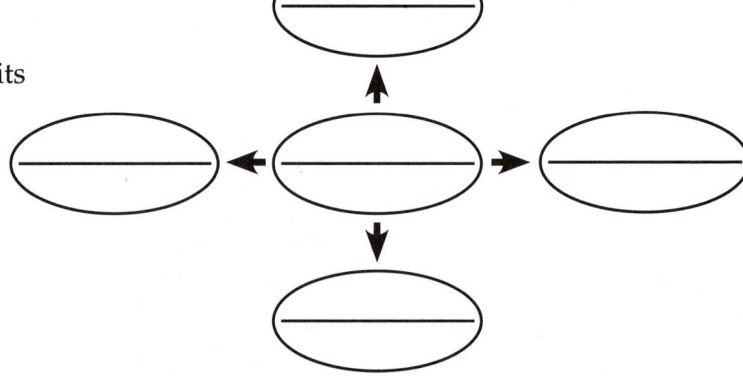

1. Why are these leadership traits important? _Student answers will vary._

Name _____ Date _____ Period _____

CHAPTER 17 Branding

Part 1: Check Your Knowledge

Matching

Write the correct term for each definition on the line provided.

Key Terms

brand equity
brand loyalty
brand name
corporate social responsibility
generic brand
intellectual property
jingle
logo
metaphor
national brand
perception
personal brand
private-label brand
service mark
tagline
trade character
trademark
value

1. Protects taglines, names, graphics, symbols, or any unique method to identify a product or company.
   trademark

2. A consumer product that lacks a widely recognized name or logo.
   generic brand

3. A tagline or slogan set to music.
   jingle

4. An animal, real or fictional person, or object used to advertise a good or service.
   trade character

5. The actions of a business to further social good.
   corporate social responsibility

Copyright Goodheart-Willcox Co., Inc. 139

6. Brand created by a manufacturer for its own products.
   national brand

7. Something that comes from a person's mind, such as an idea, invention, or process.
   intellectual property

8. The picture, design, or graphic image that represents a brand.
   logo

9. A situation in which the customer will only buy a certain brand of product.
   brand loyalty

10. The value of having a well-known brand name.
    brand equity

11. Similar to a trademark, but it identifies a service rather than a product.
    service mark

12. A phrase or sentence that summarizes some essential part of the product or business.
    tagline

13. The relative worth of something to a person.
    value

14. Products owned by and created specifically for large retailers.
    private-label brands

15. The name given to the product consisting of words, numbers, or letters that can be read and spoken.
    brand name

Chapter 17   Branding   **141**

Name _____

True or False

Decide whether each statement is true or false and enter *T* or *F* on the line provided. If the statement is false, rewrite the statement to make it true.

1. A metaphor is a word or phrase for one thing used in reference to a similar thing in order to suggest a similarity. False. A metaphor is a word or phrase for one thing used in reference to a very different thing in order to suggest a similarity.

2. Brand name is the mental picture a person has about something. False. Perception is the mental image a person has about something.

3. Consumers develop expectations for a brand based on how it is promoted and priced.
   True

4. Many companies often use product features to sell a product. True

5. Developing a unique brand always translates into a positive brand image. False. Developing a unique brand does not always translate into a positive brand image.

6. A consumer product that lacks a widely recognized name or logo is a generic brand.
   True

7. Research has shown that it costs about the same to create a new customer as it does to keep an existing one. False. Research has shown that it costs four times as much to create a new customer as it does to keep an existing one.

8. Customer experience with the brand is the main factor in brand loyalty. True

9. Generic names can be registered trademarks. False. Generic names cannot be registered trademarks.

10. Your personal brand is the sum of the differences between you and those around you.
    True

Copyright Goodheart-Willcox Co., Inc.

Part 2: Marketing by the Numbers

Negative Numbers

Business losses are written as negative numbers. For example, suppose as a marketing manager you have a $6,000 monthly marketing budget. However, in one month you had marketing expenses of $6,500. To find the difference between the budgeted and amount and the actual expenses, you would subtract $6,500 from $6,000, which results in –$500. This number is read as a negative 500 dollars. Negative numbers can also be expressed by using parentheses. In the same example, –500 dollars could also be expresses as ($500).

The following example will help you understand and work with negative numbers. Imagine that you are standing on level ground. You begin to dig a hole in the dirt using a spoon. You remove 12 spoonfuls of dirt (or –12). You then remove another 9 spoonfuls of dirt (or –9). How many spoonfuls have you removed altogether? If you said 21 spoonfuls, you would be correct (–9–12 = –21). One might say that you are 21 spoonfuls *in the hole* or a *minus* 21.

While at –21, suppose you replace 6 (or +6) spoonfuls of dirt into the hole. Now what is your status? By replacing 6 spoonfuls, you are now at *minus* 15 spoonfuls of dirt (–21 + 6 = –15).

Perform the following calculations. If you are unsure whether to add or subtract the numbers, think in terms of *spoonfuls* of dirt. Also, use estimation to help you determine whether your answer is correct. Problem one is completed for you as an example.

Problem 1			Problem 2			Problem 3	
Actual	Estimate		Actual	Estimate		Actual	Estimate
–16	–20		–27	–30		–28	–30
–45	–50		–82	–80		+74	+70
Total			Total			Total	
–61	–70		–109	–110		+46	+40

Problem 4			Problem 5			Problem 6	
Actual	Estimate		Actual	Estimate		Actual	Estimate
–83	–80		+52	+50		–124	–100
–12	–10		+44	+40		–475	–500
Total			Total			Total	
–95	–90		+96	+90		–599	–600

Problem 7			Problem 8			Problem 9	
Actual	Estimate		Actual	Estimate		Actual	Estimate
–853	–900		–736	–700		+642	+600
–153	–200		+542	+500		+378	+400
Total			Total			Total	
–1,006	–1,100		–194	–200		+1,020	+1,000

Chapter 17 Branding

Name _____

Problem 10	
Actual	Estimate
+874	+900
−268	−300
Total	
+606	+600

Problem 11	
Actual	Estimate
+690	+700
−889	−900
Total	
−199	−200

Problem 12	
Actual	Estimate
−882	−900
−457	−500
Total	
−1,339	−1,400

Problem 13	
Actual	Estimate
−1,358	−1,000
−4,752	−5,000
Total	
−6,110	−6,000

Problem 14	
Actual	Estimate
−6,308	−6,000
+7,841	+8,000
Total	
+1,533	+2,000

Problem 15	
Actual	Estimate
−5,720	−5,700
+6,100	+6,100
Total	
+380	+400

Problem 16	
Actual	Estimate
+18,932	+20,000
−27,453	−30,000
Total	
−8,521	−10,000

Problem 17	
Actual	Estimate
−56,993	−60,000
−56,993	−60,000
Total	
−113,986	−120,000

Problem 18	
Actual	Estimate
−35,627	−36,000
+35,627	+36,000
Total	
0	0

Problem 19	
Actual	Estimate
+306,771	+300,000
−388,539	−400,000
Total	
−81,768	−100,000

Problem 20	
Actual	Estimate
−892,988	−900,000
+63,176	+60,000
Total	
−829,812	−840,000

Problem 21	
Actual	Estimate
+876,452	+900,000
−1,874,025	−2,000,000
Total	
−997,573	−1,100,000

Problem 22	
Actual	Estimate
−145,963	−100,000
+238,960	+200,000
−439	0
−167,904	−200,000
+455,790	+500,000
Total	
+380,444	+400,000

Problem 23	
Actual	Estimate
+23,452	+20,000
−5,682	−6,000
−47,903	−50,000
−1,746,026	−2,000,000
+710,452	+700,000
Total	
−1,065,707	−1,300,000

Copyright Goodheart-Willcox Co., Inc.

Problem 24	
Actual	Estimate
+1,245,969	+1,000,000
−4,118,430	−4,000,000
+8,936,408	+9,000,000
+12,268,004	+12,000,000
−3,662,804	−4,000,000
Total	
+14,669,147	+14,000,000

Problem 25	
Actual	Estimate
−9,874,812	−10,000,000
−34,462	0
+12,830,958	+13,000,000
−78,924	0
+6,874,455	+7,000,000
Total	
+9,717,215	+10,000,000

Chapter 17 Branding   145

Name _____

Part 3: Demonstrate Your Knowledge

Section A

What do Boeing, Ford, and Marriott have in common? They are all large international companies named after the founders, which means the founders' names are now considered to be strong brands. In fact, these brand names are almost synonymous with their products. William Boeing started the Boeing Airplane Company. Henry Ford started the Ford Motor Company. J. Willard Marriott started the Marriott Corporation (hotels and foodservice). Answer the following questions about brand names.

1. List three brands named after people. For each one, describe the product that the brand stands for. Then, describe the image of the brand.

    Name: _Student answers will vary._____

    Product: _____

    Image: _____

    Name: _Student answers will vary._____

    Product: _____

    Image: _____

    Name: _Student answers will vary._____

    Product: _____

    Image: _____

2. List three brands that are *not* named after a person. For each brand, describe the product and the image of that brand. Then, explain why the brand name works.

    Name: _Student answers will vary._____

    Product: _____

    Image: _____

    Why name works: _____

    Name: _Student answers will vary._____

    Product: _____

    Image: _____

    Why name works: _____

    Name: _Student answers will vary._____

    Product: _____

    Image: _____

    Why name works: _____

Copyright Goodheart-Willcox Co., Inc.

Section B

Imagine that your name is the brand for a company or product. What kind of product would it be? What kind of image would it have? Describe your brand and product by answering the questions below.

1. What is your brand name? You can include other words in your brand name, such as Joseph Patel Paints or Karrie's Beauty Salon. _Student answers will vary._

2. Describe your product. _Student answers will vary._

3. Create your tagline or slogan. _Student answers will vary._

4. When people hear or see your brand name, what image do you want them to have?
   Student answers will vary.

5. What distinguishes your brand from others in the same field? _Student answers will vary._

6. How would you represent your brand when you market it? What would you wear? What would you be seen doing? _Student answers will vary._

7. Why should customers buy your brand instead of your competitors? _Student answers will vary._

8. What benefits (functional, emotional, self-expressive) does your brand offer? _Student answers will vary._

Chapter 17   Branding   **147**

Name _____

Part 4: Be Your Own Leader

Who's on My Team?

Every leader needs a great team. Your teammates want you to succeed, reach your goals, and take risks. Your team wants to help you along your leadership journey. These are the people who are, or could be, your mentors as you build your leadership skills. Use the following graphic to create your own team. Add additional boxes if you need to, but do not delete any boxes. Think about people who have qualities you want to develop in yourself. You may choose people you do or do not know personally—it is your decision. Once you have completed the graphic, answer the questions.
Student answers will vary.

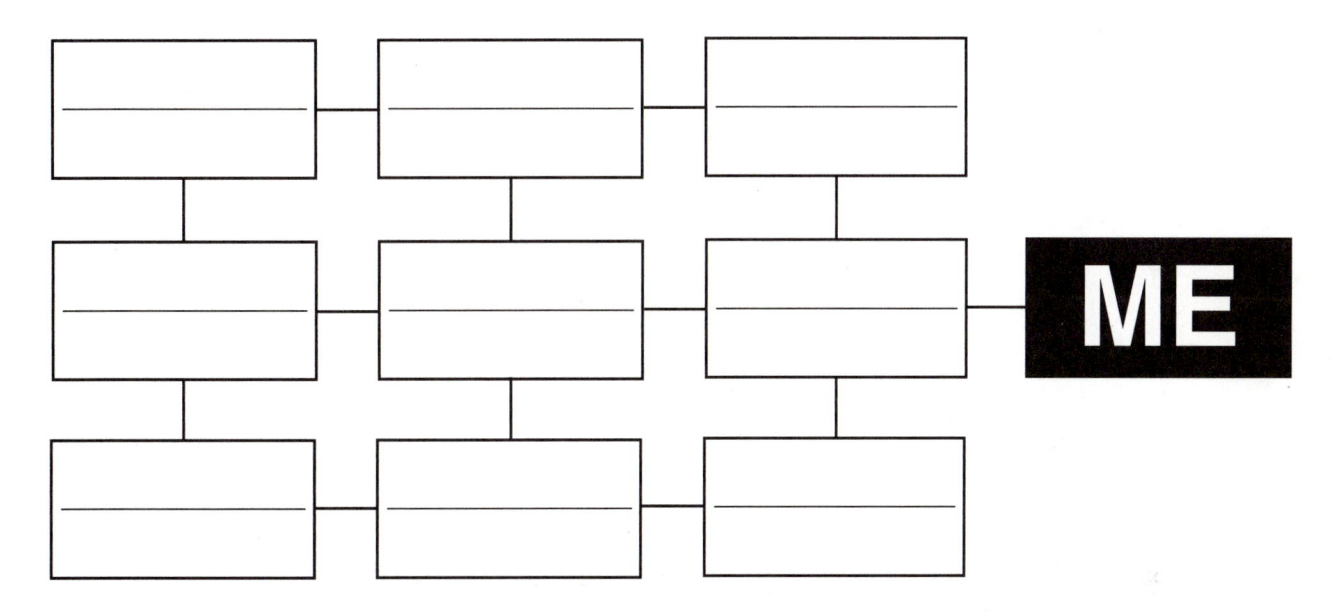

1. Why is each person on your team? Student answers will vary.
   _____
   _____
   _____

2. How might your team change over time? Student answers will vary.
   _____
   _____
   _____

3. Whose team might you be on? Student answers will vary.
   _____
   _____
   _____

Copyright Goodheart-Willcox Co., Inc.

Name _____ Date _____ Period _____

CHAPTER 18 Price

Part 1: Check Your Knowledge

Matching

Write the correct term for each definition on the line provided.

Key Terms

bait and switch
deceptive pricing
elastic demand
fixed expense
inelastic demand
law of diminishing marginal utility
list price
loss leader
manufacturer's suggested retail price (MSRP)
marginal utility
predatory pricing
price ceiling
price discrimination
price-fixing
price floor
price gouging
selling price
unit pricing
value proposition
variable expense

1. When a company sells the same product to different customers at different prices based on personal characteristics.
   price discrimination

2. Setting very low prices to remove competition, such as foreign companies that price their products below the same domestic ones to drive the domestic companies out of business.
   predatory pricing

3. Minimum prices set by the government for certain goods and services that it thinks are being priced too low.
   price floor

4. The price recommended by the manufacturer.
   manufacturer's suggested retail price (MSRP)

5. The raising of prices on certain kinds of goods to an excessively high level during an emergency.
   price gouging

Copyright Goodheart-Willcox Co., Inc. 149

6. Explains the value of the product over others that are similar.
   value proposition

7. The maximum price set by the government for certain goods and services it thinks are being priced too high.
   price ceiling

8. States that consume more units of the same product decreases the marginal utility from each unit.
   law of diminishing marginal utility

9. Expense that does and is not affected by the number of products produced or sold.
   fixed expense

10. The practice of advertising one product with the intent of persuading a customer to buy a more expensive item when they arrive in the store.
    bait and switch

11. The actual price paid for a product, after any discounts or coupons are deducted.
    selling price

12. Product demand that is not affected by price.
    inelastic demand

13. Pricing an item much lower than the current market price or the cost of acquiring the product.
    loss leader

14. The additional satisfaction gained by using one additional unit of the same product.
    marginal utility

15. Expense that changes based on the activities of the business.
    variable expense

16. The established price printed in a catalog, on a price tag, or in a price list.
    list price

17. Product demand that changes with price.
    elastic demand

18. Pricing products in a way to intentionally mislead a customer.
    deceptive pricing

19. Allows customers to compare the prices based on a standard unit of measure, such as an ounce or a pound.
    unit pricing

20. A group of competitors that get together and set the price for a specific product, which are usually high.
    price-fixing

Chapter 18   Price

Name _____

True or False

Decide whether each statement is true or false and enter *T* or *F* on the line provided. If the statement is false, rewrite the statement to make it true.

1. Some marketers use price to influence customer perception. True

2. Individual customers often place different values on the same product. True

3. The list price often includes discounts. False. The list price does not include any discounts.

4. Marketers must be sure the image created by the pricing matches the company goals outlined in the business and marketing plans. True

5. When demand rises, prices typically fall. False. When demand rises, prices also typically rise.

6. When prices for products with elastic demand are lowered, the demand rises. True

7. Only consumers are affected by unfair and unethical pricing practices. False. Both businesses and consumers are affected by unfair and unethical pricing practices.

8. There are state and federal laws that regulate pricing to prevent unfair pricing policies and practices used by some businesses. True

9. Price floors are set to help the consumers. False. Price floors are set to help the producers.

10. A surplus situation can force the government to buy the excess inventory to prevent rampant waste. True

Part 2: Marketing by the Numbers

List Price vs. Selling Price

The established price of a product is called the list price, which does *not* include any discounts. The selling price is the actual price the customer pays for a product after any discounts or coupons. Complete the table by computing the discount amount and the selling price. Remember to round to the nearest cent. The first one is completed for you as an example.

List Price ($)	Discount (%)	Discount Amount ($)	Selling Price ($)
$20.00	10%	$2.00	$18.00
29.95	15	4.49	25.46
63.99	20	12.80	51.19
89.88	60	53.93	35.95
72.99	5	3.65	69.34
84.00	25	21.00	63.00
102.00	10	10.20	91.80
159.99	20	32.00	127.99
79.98	25	20.00	59.98
24.99	10	2.50	22.49
129.98	15	19.50	110.48
162.00	50	81.00	81.00
74.99	5	3.75	71.24
48.00	20	9.60	38.40
63.98	60	38.39	25.59
249.00	40	99.60	149.40
599.99	25	150.00	449.99
600.00	10	60.00	540.00
649.98	75	487.49	162.49
829.99	5	41.50	788.49
763.88	20	152.78	611.10

Coupon or Discount?

Which is the better deal? Imagine you are a marketing manager in charge of your store's product promotions. You must decide whether to offer customers a $10 store coupon or a 20% discount. In the following table, compute the selling price after a 20% discount is applied to the list price. Then, compute the selling price for the same item after a $10.00 coupon is applied to the list price. Circle or underline the option that offers the better selling price for the customer. The first one is completed for you as an example.

List Price ($)	Discount (%)	Discount Amount ($)	Selling Price after 20% Discount ($)	Selling Price after $10 Coupon ($)
$24.99	20%	$5.00	$19.99	$14.99
63.98	20	12.80	51.18	53.98
37.00	20	7.40	29.60	27.00
43.00	20	8.60	34.40	33.00
99.98	20	20.00	79.98	89.98

Chapter 18   Price

Name _____

Part 3: Demonstrate Your Knowledge

Section A

Answer the following questions using complete sentences.

1. "The right price is the price that the customer will pay." Explain what this statement means in terms of the price of goods in the marketplace. _Student answers will vary._
_____
_____

2. Some products sell for more than they appear to be worth. Explain why this might be true and give an example. _Student answers will vary._
_____
_____

3. Some products sell for less than they appear to be worth. Explain why this might be true and give an example. _Student answers will vary._
_____
_____

Section B

Jacosta's Very Bad Day

Jacosta has to take an expensive heart medication for which her health insurance pays half of the cost. She also needs stronger contact lenses but her insurance does not cover eye care. Today, Jacosta found out that her medicine has increased in price. She also learned her rent is going up due to the increased cost of heating oil. It is time for Jacosta to rework her budget.

For Jacosta, which items have *elastic* demand? The following is a list of items Jacosta usually buys. Circle the items for which Jacosta's demand is elastic. These are the items that Jacosta might do without, or she might be able to find cheaper substitutes.

individual juice boxes	health club membership	postage
salon manicure	Premium-brand ice cream	fresh fruits and vegetables
health insurance	new tires for car	vacation cruise
car insurance	lunch at restaurants	full-price clothing
morning coffee at Starbucks	gas for car	annual dental exam

Copyright Goodheart-Willcox Co., Inc.

(Section B Continued)
Use the chart from the previous page to answer the questions below.

1. Choose one circled item from each column and list a less-expensive substitute for it. _____
   Student answers will vary.

2. What is the name of the type of demand for the uncircled products? Inelastic demand

3. What can a consumer do when the prices of the uncircled products increase? _____
   Student answers will vary.

4. How do price increases of the uncircled products affect the sales of products with elastic demand?
   Student answers will vary.

Section C

Ketchup Loyalty

Brand loyalty can lead to *inelastic* demand. Some customers will only buy a certain brand of a product. They would rather do without that product than buy another brand.

One such product is Heinz ketchup. It does not matter how its price compares with other brands, how many brands of ketchup grocers stock, or what new varieties of ketchup are introduced. Heinz continues to keep and even increase its market share. In 2012, its share of the US ketchup market was 60%.

Answer the questions that follow using complete sentences.

1. Ketchup is basically liquefied tomatoes with little to distinguish one brand from another. Why do you think people prefer and buy Heinz?
   Student answers will vary.

2. List three brand-name products that you, your family, or your friends insist on buying.
   Student answers will vary.

3. Choose one product of the products you just listed and explain why you (or they) are loyal to that brand.
   Student answers will vary.

Chapter 18   Price

Name _____

Part 4: Be Your Own Leader

Building the Foundation of Leadership

As a leader, you will be challenged. You will be challenged by those close to you, those who are not on your team, your followers, and people who want to change you. If, as a leader, you do not know what your core beliefs are, you may be persuaded to change by people with very different beliefs. Think about what is most important to you.

List your six core beliefs on the following Leadership Coat of Arms. A unique coat of arms was created by families during medieval times to identify themselves by showing a meaningful representation of what that family stood for. You can list your beliefs or draw images that illustrate your beliefs. Start by writing your name in the ribbon. Once your coat of arms is complete, share it with the class. Explain how the coat of arms you created represents you as a leader.
Student answers will vary.

Leadership Coat of Arms

3. How does the coat of arms represent you? Explain the meaning of significant elements you have included in your design.

_____
_____
_____
_____

Name _____ Date _____ Period _____

CHAPTER 19
Price Strategies

Part 1: Check Your Knowledge

Matching
Write the correct term for each definition on the line provided.

Key Terms

accounts receivable aging report
base price
break-even point
collection agency
competition-based pricing
consumer credit
cost-based pricing
cost of credit
creditor
credit bureau
credit report
credit risk
customer loyalty
debtor
debtor-creditor relationship

demand-based pricing
gross profit
installment loan
keystone pricing
markup
net profit
pricing objective
psychological pricing
return on investment (ROI)
return on marketing investment (ROMI)
total assets
trade credit
volume pricing
web-based pricing software

1. The point at which revenue from sales equals the costs.
   break-even point

2. An individual or business to whom money is owed for goods or services provided.
   creditor

3. The cash value of everything the company owns.
   total assets

4. Credit given to an individual by a retail business.
   consumer credit

Copyright Goodheart-Willcox Co., Inc.

157

5. A set of pricing techniques used to create an image of a product and to entice customers to buy.
   psychological pricing

6. The continued and regular patronage of a business when there are other places to purchase the same or similar products.
   customer loyalty

7. A company that collects past-due bills for a fee.
   collection agency

8. A pricing strategy based primarily on what the competitors charge.
   competition-based pricing

9. The goals defined in the business and marketing plans for the overall pricing policies of the company.
   pricing objectives

10. Technology that helps businesses to maximize profit by pricing products correctly.
    web-based pricing software

11. The potential of credit not being repaid.
    credit risk

12. Paid in regular payments with interest until the loan is paid in full.
    installment loan

13. A measurement showing the overall effectiveness of a marketing campaign or yearly budget.
    return on marketing investment (ROMI)

14. Doubling the total cost of a product to determine its base price.
    keystone pricing

15. Lowering list price based on the higher number of units purchased at the same time.
    volume pricing

16. What is left after all company expenses are subtracted from total revenue?
    net profit

17. A common measure of profitability based on the amount earned from the investment made in the business.
    return on investment (ROI)

18. A variable expense that influences the pricing decisions for products.
    cost of credit

19. The amount added to the cost of a product to determine the base price.
    markup

Chapter 19   Price Strategies

Name _____

20. Granting a line of credit to another business for a short period of time to purchase its goods and services.
    trade credit

21. A method that uses the cost of the product to set the base price.
    cost-based pricing

22. A record of a business or person's credit history and financial behavior.
    credit report

23. The general price at which the company expects to sell the product.
    base price

24. A pricing strategy based on what customers are willing to pay.
    demand-based pricing

25. A private firm that mains consumer credit data and provides credit information to business for a fee.
    accounts receivable

26. A document that shows when accounts receivables are due as well as the length of time accounts have been outstanding.
    aging report

27. A legal relationship existing between a debtor and a creditor based on good faith that both parties will uphold their end of the agreement.
    debtor-creditor relationship

28. The amount of profit before subtracting the cost of goods sold.
    gross profit

29. An individual or business who owes money for good or services provided.
    debtor

True or False

Decide whether each statement is true or false and enter T or F on the line provided. If the statement is false, rewrite the statement to make it true.

1. Pricing objectives rarely change. False. Pricing objectives change and should be revised regularly.

2. Increasing market share by gaining more customers is one way to maximize sales.
   True

3. Gross profit is the amount of profit after subtracting the costs of doing business.
   False. Gross profit is the amount of profit before subtracting the costs of doing business.

4. A high ROI typically indicates a profitable company. True

5. The break-even point is often expressed as the number of items that must be sold to recover the money spent to create or buy them. True

6. Using a percentage markup is the most common way to determine a base price. True

7. Most retail businesses do *not* use the percentage markup method because it does not guarantee a consistent level of profit. False. Most retail businesses use the percentage markup method because it guarantees a consistent level of profit.

8. Demand-based pricing is a long-term pricing strategy. False. Demand-based pricing is a short-term pricing strategy.

9. Competition-based pricing does *not* take into account the cost of producing the product and may not provide enough, or any, profit. True

10. Even pricing conveys quality. True

Chapter 19   Price Strategies

Name _____

Part 2: Marketing by the Numbers

Break-Even Point

The *break-even point* is the point at which the revenue from sales equals cost of selling the products. At this point, the company is not losing or making money. This is known as *breaking even*. Once the break-even point is reached, all the additional revenue is profit. The number of items that must be sold to break even can be calculated. The break-even formula for a retail situation follows.

$$\frac{\text{(cost per unit)} \times \text{(number of units purchased)}}{\text{selling price}} = \text{break-even point}$$

Using the formula above, complete the following table by calculating the cost of all units and the break-even point for each. The first one is completed for you as an example.

\multicolumn{5}{c	}{Break-Even Point}
Cost per Unit	Number of Units Purchased	Cost of All Units	Selling Price	Break-Even Point (Number of Units Must Be Sold)
$2.50	100	$250	$5.00	50
7.25	200	1,450	14.50	100
12.00	250	3,000	20.00	150
22.50	150	3,375	25.00	135
15.00	225	3,375	25.00	135
22.50	150	3,375	45.00	75
2.25	1,000	2,250	5.00	450
6.80	500	3,400	10.00	340
7.23	1,000	7,230	10.00	723
12.96	1,500	19,440	20.00	972
6.62	2,000	13,240	10.00	1,324
144.50	400	57,800	200.00	289
89.40	500	44,700	150.00	298
62.50	150	9,375	75.00	125
108.00	50	5,400	150.00	36
450.00	50	22,500	900.00	25
164.00	100	16,400	200.00	82
56.50	150	8,475	75.00	113
147.00	100	14,700	175.00	84
80.00	30	2,400	200.00	12

Copyright Goodheart-Willcox Co., Inc.

Part 3: Demonstrate Your Knowledge

Pricing Techniques

The following is a list of pricing techniques. Sort them into their proper category of B2B or B2C by listing them under the proper column in the following table.

cash discount
even pricing
odd pricing
prestige pricing
price lining
promotional discount
promotional pricing
quantity discount
seasonal discount,
trade discount
unit pricing

Pricing Techniques	
Psychological Pricing (B2C)	**Discount Pricing (B2B)**
price lining, odd pricing, even pricing, unit pricing, prestige pricing, promotional pricing	cash discount, promotional discount, trade discount, quantity discount, seasonal discount

B2C Psychological Pricing

In the consumer market, psychological pricing techniques are often used. Some common B2C psychological pricing techniques include odd, even, and prestige pricing; price lining; BOGO; and bundling. In the following examples, write the pricing technique in the space provided for each example. Some examples use more than one technique.

1. Joy 1000, a perfume by French designer Jean Patou, is priced at $190.
   even, prestige

2. Sign in the window of Sole Mates shoe store reads, "All shoes always $29.99."
   odd

3. The old Sears and Roebucks catalog listed three price/quality levels: good (least expensive), better (medium price), best (most expensive).
   price lining

4. The rooms at the Dolley Madison Inn are priced at $400 per night.
   even, prestige

5. Every book in the sale catalog of Edward R. Hamilton is priced at $1.99, $2.99, or $3.99.
   odd

6. A house on Silver Lake was listed for sale at $2.2 million.
   even, prestige

7. The same house described in the previous example was damaged by a hailstorm. It was advertised as "Reduced! Now only $1,999,999!"
   odd

Chapter 19 Price Strategies **163**

Name _____

8. Every six months, Ray's Tires and Retreads runs a newspaper ad with the headline, "Buy one, get one 50% off.

   BOGO

9. A retailer that sells stereo systems offers a basic system for $500, a system with several optional components for $750, and a top quality system for $1,000.

   even, price lining

10. A local cable company that offers cable, Internet, and phone service will discount the monthly rate if all three services are purchased.

    bundling

Part 4: Be Your Own Leader

Where Do I Rank?

Review the leadership qualities listed in Column 1 of the chart below. At the bottom of Column 1, write three additional qualities of your own. Next, write your definition of each leadership quality in the shaded box provided. Then, for each example, rank yourself by placing an *X* in the column that best represents you. If you checked *Pretty Good, Need to Focus*, or *I Need Help*, create a plan for how you will improve, using the chart on the next page. Student answers will vary.

Leadership Quality	Your Definition	Definitely Excel in This Area	Pretty Good in This Area	Need To Focus on This Area	I Need Help in This Area
Enthusiasm					
Motivation					
Attitude					
Communication					
Creativity					
Integrity					
Tact					
Courage					
Dependability					
Share credit					
Accountable					
Problem Solving					
Your own:					
Your own:					
Your own:					

Chapter 19 Price Strategies

165

Name _____

Plan for Improvement

List the leadership quality on the left and your plan for improvement on your right. Use complete sentences. Set a goal for when your plan will be accomplished. Student answers will vary.

Quality to improve	Plan for Improvement/Goal

Name _____ Date _____ Period _____

CHAPTER 20 Place

Part 1: Check Your Knowledge

Matching

Write the correct term for each definition on the line provided.

Key Terms

agent
agent/broker channel
brick-and-mortar
bulk-breaking
channel of distribution
common carrier
direct channel
e-tailer
exclusive distribution
export management company
freight forwarder
indirect channel
industrial good
intensive distribution
intermediary
pipeline
private carrier
private warehouse
public warehouse
retailer channel
selective distribution
supply chain
supply chain management
supply chain manager
transportation
wholesaler channel

1. Coordinating the events happening throughout the supply chain.
   supply chain management

2. Places product in every potential sales situation possible.
   intensive distribution

3. The process of separating a large quantity of goods into smaller quantities for resale.
   bulk-breaking

4. The path a product takes from the producer, to a wholesaler, and the retailer before reaching the end user.
   wholesaler channel

Copyright Goodheart-Willcox Co., Inc.

167

5. The path that goods take through the supply chain.
   channel of distribution

6. The term for a physical store.
   brick-and-mortar

7. The path of selling goods from the producer to the retailer, then from the retailer to the consumer.
   retailer channel

8. A line of connected pipes that are used for carrying liquids and gases over a long distance.
   pipeline

9. The person who coordinates and monitors all the activities from the building of the product to delivery to the end user.
   supply chain manager

10. An independent company that provides support services, such as warehousing, shipping, insuring, and billing, on behalf of the business.
    export management company

11. A retailer that sells through the Internet.
    e-tailer

12. The businesses, people, and activities involved in turning raw materials into products and delivering them to end users.
    supply chain

13. The path of selling goods or services directly from the manufacturer to the end user without using intermediaries.
    direct channel

14. A company that organizes shipments.
    freight forwarder

15. Goods used in the production of other goods or consumed by a business.
    industrial goods

16. Occurs when there is only one channel member, or distributor of products, in a market area.
    exclusive distribution

17. Uses intermediaries to get the product from the manufacturer to the end users.
    indirect channel

18. Someone working on the behalf of another party.
    agent

Chapter 20   Place

Name _____

19. Owned by a company for storage of their own goods.
    private warehouses

20. Selecting the specific places that the manufacturer or wholesaler wants the product to be sold.
    selective distribution

21. The physical movement of products through the channel of distribution.
    transportation

22. The person or business in between the manufacturers or producers and the end users.
    intermediary

23. An independent trucking company.
    common carrier

24. The path of selling in which the producer hires an agent to sell to the wholesaler.
    agent/broker channel

25. Offers storage space to any company.
    public warehouse

True or False

Decide whether each statement is true or false and enter *T* or *F* on the line provided. If the statement is false, rewrite the statement to make it true.

1. Wholesalers purchase large amounts of goods directly from retailers. _False. Wholesalers purchase large amounts of goods directly from manufacturers._

2. An agent may be hired by either the buyer or the seller. _True_

3. The facilitating function is physically moving products from the manufacturers to distributors, retailers, or end users. _False. The logistics function is physically moving products from the manufacturers to distributors, retailers, or end users._

4. The physical distribution actually gives the end user possession of the goods. _True_

5. Trucking is the most common method of distribution in the United States. _True_

6. A private carrier is a company that transports goods for other companies. _False. A private carrier is a company that transports its own goods._

7. Independent trucking companies can be called contract carriers. _True_

8. Low-value, high-weight items are often shipped by air. _False. High-value, low-weight items are often shipped by air._

9. Marketers working for companies that buy, sell, or distribute products globally have more complex place decisions. _True_

10. Marketers working for companies that buy, sell, or distribute products globally have simple place decisions. _False. Marketers working for companies that buy, sell, or distribute products globally have more complex place decisions._

Chapter 20 Place

Name _____

Part 2: Marketing by the Numbers

Shipping Costs

Marketers who work for retail or shipping businesses often have to send packages of varying weights to different destinations. The following chart shows the shipping rates for a physical transportation carrier called Careful Carrier. The listed rates are from Zone 1 to the different zones indicated. Use the information in the chart to answer the questions that follow.

	Careful Carrier Shipping Rates					
Weight (in lb)	Zone 1 ($)	Zone 2 ($)	Zone 3 ($)	Zone 4 ($)	Zone 5 ($)	Zone 6 ($)
16	72.50	79.75	92.25	93.25	93.75	98.50
17	73.75	81.00	94.75	95.75	96.25	101.00
18	75.00	82.25	97.25	98.25	98.75	103.50
19	76.25	83.50	99.75	100.75	101.25	106.00
20	77.50	84.75	102.25	103.25	103.75	108.50
21	78.75	86.00	104.75	105.75	106.25	111.00
22	80.00	87.25	107.25	108.25	108.75	113.50
23	81.25	88.50	109.75	110.75	111.25	116.00
24	82.50	89.75	112.25	113.25	113.75	118.50

Determine the rates for shipping the following packages:

1. From Zone 1 to Zone 2, 22 lb $87.25
2. From Zone 1 to Zone 3, 19 lb $99.75
3. From Zone 1 to Zone 6, 20 lb $108.50
4. From Zone 1 to Zone 5, 16 lb $93.75
5. From Zone 1 to Zone 2, 18 lb $82.25
6. From Zone 1 to Zone 4, 21 lb $105.75
7. From Zone 1 to Zone 5, 24 lb $113.75

Suppose you have a 21 lb package to send. Calculate the difference in rate between sending it to the first zone listed versus the second zone listed. An example has been completed for you.

Zone 1 vs. Zone 4
$105.75 − $78.75 = $27.00

1. Zone 2 vs. Zone 6 $111.00 − $86.00 = $25.00
2. Zone 4 vs. Zone 5 $106.25 − 105.75 = $0.50
3. Zone 3 vs. Zone 6 $111.00 − $104.75 = $6.25
4. Zone 5 vs. Zone 6 $111.00 − 106.25 = $4.75

Copyright Goodheart-Willcox Co., Inc.

Calculate the difference in rate for sending the following packages to the listed zones. An example has been completed for you.

Zone 3, 16 lb vs. 24 lb
$112.25 − $92.25 = $20.00

1. Zone 1, 17 lb vs. 20 lb $77.50 − $73.75 = $3.75
2. Zone 5, 20 lb vs. 22 lb $108.75 − $103.75 = $5.00
3. Zone 2, 18 lb vs. 24 lb $89.75 − $82.25 = $7.50

Chapter 20   Place   173

Name _____

Part 3: Demonstrate Your Knowledge

Physical Distribution Simplified

Students from a nearby high school are doing a social-studies unit on products in their local stores. Imagine you are a marketing manager who is invited to help the students understand how goods get from one place to another. You will help the students understand the general concept of physical distribution. Use the following suggestions and questions to demonstrate the supply chain and possible channels of distribution for these items: raw materials to factory; finished goods from the factory to a warehouse; and finished goods from the warehouse to the stores.

1. Why is distribution necessary for many businesses? Develop a creative way to help students understand why distribution is important. What props could you use to illustrate the concepts involved in physical distribution?
   Student answers will vary. _____
   _____

2. Present the six modes of transportation. What can you show students to help them understand and keep them interested?

   Road Student answers will vary. _____

   Rail _____

   Air _____

   Water _____

   Pipeline _____

   Digital _____

3. Name a product that you will use to illustrate a channel of distribution. Why did you choose this product? Develop a channel of distribution with your students for the product you chose.
   Student answers will vary. _____
   _____

4. Summarize the role of channel management in physical distribution of a product.
   Student answers will vary. _____
   _____

5. How will you determine what the students actually learned?
   Student answers will vary. _____
   _____

Copyright Goodheart-Willcox Co., Inc.

Part 4: Be Your Own Leader

Put Leadership into Practice, Part I

You have learned a lot about leadership. Now it is time to put your knowledge into practice. Choose an activity for which you have a passion or great interest. You may consider a charity or community service activity, an advertising campaign for your school-based enterprise, a written event for your CTSO, a social activity for your class, a speaker on a specific topic, or some other activity. In this chapter and the next, you will plan, implement, and reflect on an activity of your choice. Start by completing the activities below.

1. Name(s) of group members Student answers will vary.

2. Activity Student answers will vary.

3. Date(s) of activity Student answers will vary.

4. Activity description (describe the activity in detail). Student answers will vary.

5. Why are you doing this activity? Student answers will vary.

6. What do you hope to achieve through this activity? Student answers will vary.

7. Complete the following chart to note the tasks, persons responsible, resources needed, due dates, and completion dates. Student answers will vary.

Task	Person Responsible	Resources Needed	Due Date	Completion Date

Complete the activity you planned above. In the next chapter, you will reflect on your activity.

Name _____ Date _____ Period _____

CHAPTER 21: Purchasing and Inventory Control

Part 1: Check Your Knowledge

Matching

Write the correct term for each definition on the line provided.

Key Terms

80/20 inventory rule
buffer stock
economy of scale
electronic data interchange (EDI)
external theft
internal theft
inventory
inventory management
inventory shrinkage
invoice
just-in-time (JIT) inventory-control system
manual-tag system
packing slip
periodic inventory-control system
perpetual inventory-control system
physical inventory
point-of-sale (POS) software
product specification sheet
purchase order (PO)
quality control
radio frequency identification (RFID)
receiving record
reorder point
stockout
turnover rate
unit-control system

1. The activity of checking goods as they are produced or received to ensure the quality meets expectations.
   quality control

2. The number of times inventory has been sold during a time period, usually one year.
   turnover rate

3. The form a buyer sends to the vendor to officially place an order.
   purchase order

4. A system that uses computer chips attached to inventory items and radio frequency receivers to track inventory.
   radio frequency identification (RFID)

Copyright Goodheart-Willcox Co., Inc. 175

5. Committed by employees of a store, a supplier, or a delivery company.
   internal theft

6. Keeping a minimal amount of production materials or sales inventory on hand at all times.
   just-in-time (JIT) inventory-control system

7. Uses a visual determination to decide when more stock is needed.
   unit-control system

8. Running out of stock.
   stockout

9. The vendor bill requesting payment for goods shipped or services provided.
   invoice

10. The decrease in unit cost of a product resulting from large scale manufacturing operations.
    economy of scale

11. The standard transfer of electronic data for business transactions between organizations.
    electronic data interchange (EDI)

12. A document that lists the contents of the box or container.
    packing slip

13. Additional stock kept above the minimum amount required to meet forecasted sales.
    buffer stock

14. Tracks sales by removing price tags when the products are sold.
    manual-tag system

15. The difference between the perpetual inventory and the actual physical inventory.
    inventory shrinkage.

16. Stealing by people who are not employed or otherwise associated with the retailer.
    external theft

17. Technology that electronically records each sale when it happens by scanning product bar codes.
    point-of-sale (POS) software

18. The process of buying and storing inventory while keeping the costs associated with the inventory low.
    inventory management

19. Puts a control in place to trigger placing an order before the inventory gets too low.
    reorder point

Chapter 21   Purchasing and Inventory Control

Name _____

20. The assortment or selection of items that a business has in stock.
    inventory

21. An actual count of all items in inventory at that time.
    physical inventory

22. States that 80 percent of the sales for a business come from 20 percent of its inventory.
    80/20 inventory rule

23. Involves taking a physical count of merchandise at regular periods, such as weekly or monthly.
    periodic inventory-control system

24. Provides product facts including sizes, colors, materials, and weights.
    product specification sheet

25. A method of counting inventory that shows the quantity on hand at all times.
    perpetual inventory-control system

True or False

Decide whether each statement is true or false and enter *T* or *F* on the line provided. If the statement is false, rewrite the statement to make it true.

1. Much of the purchasing process takes place electronically to maximize efficiency and easily maintain records. True

2. After placing orders for merchandise, buyers must study the target market. False. Before placing orders for merchandise, buyers must study the target market.

3. If a business has been in operation for a few years, it is important to use actual sales history to determine inventory needs. True

4. Most vendors offer quantity discounts, or a reduced per-item price based on the quantity purchased, to encourage larger orders. True

5. A receiving record is the form on which all merchandise received is listed when it is packed and shipped from the business. False. A receiving record is the form on which all merchandise received is listed as it comes into the place of business.

6. Computerized inventory-control systems have nothing to do with EDI. False. Computerized inventory-control systems are an important part of EDI.

7. Lead time is the total time it takes from placing an order until it is received. True

8. Buffer stock is the necessary extra stock of products that sell more in certain seasons.
False. Anticipation stock is the necessary extra stock of products that sell more in certain seasons.

9. It is not necessarily important to conduct a physical inventory once or twice a year.
False. No matter which inventory-control system a business uses, it is important to conduct a physical inventory once or twice a year.

10. Most retail businesses use cash registers with point-of-sale software. True

Chapter 21   Purchasing and Inventory Control

Name _____

Part 2: Marketing by the Numbers

Turnover Rate

Turnover rate is the number of times the average inventory on hand is sold and completely replaced in a specific time period, usually one year. Turnover rate is also called *turnover ratio*. It is a measure of how fast the goods are being sold. The formula for calculating a turnover rate is

$$\frac{\text{Cost of Goods Sold}}{\text{Average Inventory Value}} = \text{Turnover rate}$$

Complete the following table to find stock turnover rates in different situations. The period of time is one year. Use rounding to calculate your estimate. The first problem is completed for you as an example.

Cost of Goods Sold ($)	Average Value of Inventory ($)	Estimate	Turnover Rate
$25,080	$5,100	25,000/5,000 = 5	5
600,000	90,000	600,000/90,000 = 6.667	7
508,000	19,675	500,000/20,000 = 25	25
1,990,000	10,000	2,000,000/10,000 = 200	200
1,099,892	50,842	1,000,000/50,000 = 20	20
7,895,070	60,945	8,000,000/60,000 = 133.333	133
49,395,328	100,964	50,000,000/100,000 = 500	500
99,938,250	395,753	100,000,000/400,000 = 250	250
501,204,124	79,867,354	500,000,000/80,000,000 = 6.25	6
696,003,000	80,000,375	700,000,000/80,000,000 = 8.75	9

Copyright Goodheart-Willcox Co., Inc.

Part 3: Demonstrate Your Knowledge

Inventory

The following is a list of some types of retail stores. Respond to the questions using these stores and the inventory that they carry as a guide.

bakery
car dealership
clothing store
fine jewelry store
florist
hardware store
newsstand
pharmacy
sporting goods
supermarket
traditional menswear
shoe boutique

1. List five stores that stock perishable items. For each store type, list at least one specific perishable item.
   Student answers will vary.

2. For the stores that carry perishable items, what happens if the stock turnover is low?
   Student answers will vary.

3. Some clothing stores have large areas full of marked-down merchandise, often long after the season's sales. What does this situation say about the store's inventory planning?
   Student answers will vary.

4. What effect do the mark-down racks have on the new merchandise a clothing store carries?
   Student answers will vary.

5. Describe ways in which to handle unsold stock rather than discounting it.
   Student answers will vary.

Chapter 21 Purchasing and Inventory Control **181**

Name _____

6. Name five products that tend to have a high turnover rate.
   Student answers will vary.

7. Give reasons to support your answer for question #6.
   Student answers will vary.

8. Name five products that tend to have a low turnover rate.
   Student answers will vary.

9. Give reasons to support your answer for question #8.
   Student answers will vary.

10. For the products that you named in question #8, provide suggestions on ways to increase the turnover rates for these products.
    Student answers will vary.

Part 4: Be Your Own Leader

Put Leadership into Practice, Part 2

In the previous chapter, you planned and implemented an activity that you were responsible for leading. All good leaders reflect on their experiences to plan for improving any future activities they lead. Answer the following questions to help you improve your leadership skills.

1. Activity completed _Student answers will vary._

2. Team member(s) _Student answers will vary._

3. What went well? Be specific. _Student answers will vary._
   Student answers will vary.

4. What issues and/or opportunities did you experience? Why?
   Student answers will vary.

5. If other members were part of your leadership team, what did they do well?
   Student answers will vary.

6. If other members were part of your leadership team, what could they do to improve?
   Student answers will vary.

7. Were you well prepared? Why or why not?
   Student answers will vary.

8. Now that you have completed the activity, what would you do differently next time you lead a similar activity?
   Student answers will vary.

9. What did you learn from the experience that can help you in the future?
   Student answers will vary.

10. What leadership traits did you have to use to accomplish the activity?
    Student answers will vary.

11. Review your task list. Were there any tasks not completed on time or left uncompleted? Why or why not?
    Student answers will vary.

Name _____ Date _____ Period _____

CHAPTER 22
Communication Process

Part 1: Check Your Knowledge

Matching

Write the correct term for each definition on the line provided.

Key Terms

active listening
active reading
barrier
body language
channel
communication process
decoding
diversity
empathy
encoding
feedback
four Cs of writing
memo
multicultural society
multigenerational
nonverbal communication

passive listening
prejudice
reading for detail
receiver
receiving barrier
report
scanning
sender
sending barrier
skimming
telephone etiquette
transmission
verbal communication
writing process
written communication

1. Communication through facial expressions, gestures, body movements, and body position.
   body language

2. A set of sequential stages for each writing task.
   writing process

3. Can occur when the sender says or does something that causes the receiver to tune out the message.
   sending barrier

4. Having people who are different races or who have different cultures in a group or organization.
   diversity

Copyright Goodheart-Willcox Co., Inc.   183

5. Translating a message into terms that the receiver can understand.
   decoding

6. The act of sending a message.
   transmission

7. Anything that prevents clear, effective communication.
   barrier

8. The recording of written words.
   written communication

9. A brief message sent to someone within an organization.
   memo

10. Speaking.
    verbal communication

11. One who does not pay attention to what is being said.
    passive listener

12. Moving the eyes quickly down the page to find specific words and phrases.
    scanning

13. A longer discussion of a topic presented in a structured format.
    report

14. People of different generations who are in the same place, such as living in the same home or working together in the same office.
    multigenerational

15. The person who gets the message.
    receiver

16. The path a message follows.
    communication process

17. How the message is transmitted, such as face-to-face conversation, telephone, e-mail, text, or any other appropriate vehicle.
    channel

18. The response of the receiver to a message; it also concludes the communication cycle.
    feedback

19. Clear, concise, courteous, and correct communication.
    four Cs of writing

Chapter 22   Communication Process

Name _____

20. Involves reading all of the words and phrases and considering their meanings.
    reading for detail

21. The process of seeing things from the point of view of another person.
    empathy

22. Using good manners on the telephone.
    telephone etiquette

23. A society consisting of people from many cultures.
    multicultural society

24. The person who has a message to communicate.
    sender

25. Quickly glancing over the entire document to identify the main ideas.
    skimming

26. The process of turning the idea for a message into symbols that are communicated to others.
    encoding

27. Can occur when the receiver says or does something that causes a message to not be received as intended.
    receiving barrier

28. Type of listening in which the listener is thinking about what is being said.
    active listening

29. A feeling of like or dislike for someone, especially when it is not reasonable or logical.
    prejudice

30. Takes place when the reader is thinking about what he or she is reading.
    active reading

Copyright Goodheart-Willcox Co., Inc.

True or False

Decide whether each statement is true or false and enter *T* or *F* on the line provided. If the statement is false, rewrite the statement to make it true.

1. The sender of a message can be one person, a group of people, a business, or another type of organization. **True**

2. When you create a message, you are decoding it. **False. When you create a message, you are encoding it.**

3. We live in a global society in which the market is diverse. **True**

4. Most receiving barriers cannot be overcome. **False. Most receiving barriers can be overcome.**

5. While listening is an innate ability, hearing is a conscious action. **False. While hearing is an innate ability, listening is a conscious action.**

6. The appearance of your written documents is not as important as the content. **False. The appearance of your written documents is just as important as the content.**

7. The company letterhead often includes the logo of the company. **True**

8. An e-mail is *not* considered a form of business communication. **False. An e-mail may also be considered a form of business communication.**

9. Planning is the most important stage of preparing any kind of report. **True**

10. Nonverbal communication refers to words, as opposed to actions, that send messages. **False. Nonverbal communication refers to actions, as opposed to words, that send messages.**

Chapter 22   Communication Process

Name _____

Part 2: Marketing by the Numbers

Using Averages

In general terms, an average is a number that represents the typical value of a set of numbers. In mathematical terms, an average is calculated by adding quantities together and then dividing the total by the number of quantities. Averages are very useful in marketing. A common use for averages is to describe the typical monthly sales of a business. To obtain average monthly sales, add the sales for 12 months, then divide by 12. Compute the average monthly sales for each store listed in the table that follows. Calculate an estimate first. Round your answers to the highest place value. The month of January is completed for you as an example.

Monthly and Average Sales (in Dollars)				
Month	Parva's Superette Actual Sales	Parva's Estimate (Average)	Ruis's Restaurant Actual Sales	Ruis's Estimate (Average)
January	$45,246	$50,000	$83,883	$80,000
February	34,871	30,000	84,549	80,000
March	64,982	60,000	80,402	80,000
April	41,082	40,000	82,361	80,000
May	66,984	70,000	78,774	80,000
June	73,951	70,000	44,229	40,000
July	76,905	80,000	24,382	20,000
August	75,354	80,000	20,467	20,000
September	63,824	60,000	34,001	30,000
October	59,204	60,000	43,987	40,000
November	43,381	40,000	82,126	80,000
December	39,984	40,000	81,998	80,000
Total Year Sales	685,768	680,000	741,159	710,000
Average Monthly Sales	57,147	56,667	61,763	59,167

Copyright Goodheart-Willcox Co., Inc.

Monthly and Average Sales (in Dollars)				
Month	Lenny's Laundromat Actual Sales	Lenny's Estimate (Average)	Jenny's Jewelry Actual Sales	Jenny's Estimate (Average)
January	$24,452	$20,000	$50,365	$50,000
February	28,496	30,000	104,624	100,000
March	27,871	30,000	48,302	50,000
April	28,934	30,000	43,873	40,000
May	30,307	30,000	47,004	50,000
June	35,004	40,000	41,526	40,000
July	42,927	40,000	40,983	40,000
August	41,872	40,000	41,604	40,000
September	36,793	40,000	43,892	40,000
October	22,364	20,000	48,128	50,000
November	26,846	30,000	78,352	80,000
December	25,519	30,000	102,781	100,000
Total Sales	371,385	380,000	691,434	680,000
Average Monthly Sales	30,949	31,667	57,620	56,667

Chapter 22   Communication Process   **189**

Name _____

Part 3: Demonstrate Your Knowledge

Nonverbal Messages in Sales

The following scenarios describe several B2B marketing situations. Read each one carefully. Then, interpret the nonverbal messages by answering the questions in complete sentences. Keep in mind, body language and specific items can be deliberately chosen to create an image, just as words do. They may not, however, reflect the truth.

1. Cesar is making his first call on a prospective customer. As Cesar explains his company's services, the customer leans back in his chair, arms folded across his chest. His eyes look past Cesar to the open door beyond. What is the customer's body language saying? Is there another interpretation? If yes, what might it be?

   Student answers will vary.
   _____

2. On Cesar's next call, the prospective customer leans forward in her chair and makes eye contact with Cesar. What is this customer's body language saying? Is there another interpretation? If yes, what might it be?

   Student answers will vary.
   _____

3. Della is making her first visit to a prospective customer. This customer stays seated behind her desk. Although there is a visitor's chair, she does not invite Della to sit down. What is this customer's body language saying?

   Student answers will vary.
   _____

4. On Della's next call, the potential customer comes out from behind the desk to greet her. He invites her to sit in a comfortable chair and seats himself in a chair nearby. What is this customer's body language saying? Is there another interpretation? If yes, what might it be?

   Student answers will vary.
   _____

5. One of Angelo's regular customers has a white and chrome office décor. No personal photographs or other items are visible. What message does this office send? Is there another interpretation? If yes, what might it be?

   Student answers will vary.
   _____

Copyright Goodheart-Willcox Co., Inc.

6. Another of Angelo's customers has an office with wood furniture and blue carpeting. She has many family photos visible, an unusual container holding her pens, and a tennis trophy on her desk. What message does this office send? Is there another interpretation? If yes, what might it be?

   Student answers will vary.

7. Rahel is applying for an internship at a local advertising agency. When she shakes hands with Mr. Hale, the owner, she notices his large diamond ring and monogrammed cuffs on his shirt. Mr. Hale has a large mahogany desk and a photo on the wall shows him standing beside an expensive sports car. What message does Mr. Hale want these items to send? Is the message necessarily accurate?

   Student answers will vary.

8. In one company, most of the employees dress casually in shirts with pants or skirts. The supervisor of one department always wears business suits. Another supervisor dresses casually. What message does each supervisor send through his or her dress? How might this affect the employees?

   Student answers will vary.

9. Danisse's coworker, Carolie, wears very strong perfume—so strong that Danisse tries to avoid being near her. The perfume bothers other people, too. Once, Danisse heard the office manager asking Carolie not to wear such a strong fragrance. What message might Carolie be sending? Is there another interpretation? If yes, what might it be?

   Student answers will vary.

Marketing and Feedback

Feedback is the sixth element in the communication process. Read the following scenario and answer the question using complete sentences.

1. The Aflac duck pops up everywhere in advertising. Most viewers just see a duck. People in the market for insurance, however, also learn a company name, Aflac, which stands for The American Family Life Assurance Company. During the first four years of the Aflac duck campaign, Aflac sales doubled. Two of the three largest corporations, Walmart and UPS, began offering Aflac insurance. Identify the feedback you see in this form of messaging. How did marketers know the Aflac duck campaign was successful?

   Student answers will vary.

Chapter 22   Communication Process

Name _____

Part 4: Be Your Own Leader

Types of Behaviors

People in a group may exhibit different types of behaviors. As a leader, you will have to deal with each of the following types of behavior at some point in your career. After reading and understanding the differences among the behaviors, read the case study and use these behaviors to answer the questions that follow. You may need to complete the questions on a separate piece of paper.

- **Passive** behavior occurs when a person hopes that the problem or issue will simply resolve itself. A passive person does little or nothing to solve the problem or issue.
- **Aggressive** behavior occurs when a person puts pressure on others to respond in the way he or she wants the person to respond. An aggressive person argues frequently and provides reasons why something will not work.
- **Passive-aggressive** behavior occurs when a person is indirectly aggressive. A passive-aggressive person may refuse to complete a task they have agreed to, may display anger over something different, or create dissent in the group.
- **Assertive** behavior occurs when a person holds themselves and others accountable for a problem or an issue. An assertive person may try to take leadership of a group in order to solve the problem.

Case Study

You are asked to create a marketing plan for a new client. The client is expecting a draft of the marketing plan in one week, with the final plan completed in two weeks. As a marketing manager, your boss has assigned you to lead the group that will be working on the marketing plan. Five people with whom you have not worked with before are also assigned to the group. The group is composed of peers; no one has a higher position than any other member in your regular work positions.

Due to the pressure of completing the plan in such a short time, the group members begin to display some of the described behaviors. For example, Corrine continues to remind the group that she already has a full load of work waiting for her at her desk and does not have time to work on this project. Anjali, when asked to bring a list of ideas back on the second day, spends five minutes explaining why he was not able to complete the assignment. After the first day, Jermaine asks the CEO why you were chosen as the group leader when he feels that he is the most qualified. Shelby continuously interrupts and tries to steer the group in a new direction. By the end of the second day, little progress has been made on the marketing plan. As the leader, what are you going to do?

1. Choose one of the group members. Write a role-play of what you would say to that person and how they will respond as you attempt to resolve the issue(s).

   Student answers will vary.

2. Describe how you will get the group to work together to accomplish the goal of creating a marketing plan. As a leader, what specifically will you say to the group to get them to work together?

Student answers will vary.

3. Develop a rough outline of what you will need to accomplish in the first week and the second week. How will you divide the work to get the marketing plan finished on time?

Student answers will vary.

Name _____ Date _____ Period _____

CHAPTER 23 Promotions

Part 1: Check Your Knowledge

Matching

Write the correct term for each definition on the line provided.

Key Terms

AIDA
blog
circulation
direct mail
electronic promotion
event marketing
institutional promotion
integrated marketing communications (IMC)
mobile app
personal selling
persuasion
product promotion
promotional campaign
pull promotional concept
push promotional concept
preselling
press conference
press kit
press release
quick response (QR) codes
search engine optimization (SEO)
uniform resource locator (URL)
viral marketing

1. Involves taking the product directly to the customer.
   push promotional concept

2. Any promotion that uses the Internet or other technology like smartphones.
   electronic promotion

3. Information about products that customers or viewers are compelled to pass along to others.
   viral marketing

4. A website in a journal format created by a person or organization.
   blog

5. A packet of information distributed to the media about a new business opening or other major business events.
   press kit

Copyright Goodheart-Willcox Co., Inc. 193

6. Stands for customer attention, interest, desire, and action.
   AIDA

7. The coordination of marketing communications to achieve a specific goal.
   promotional campaign

8. Uses logic to change a belief or get people to take a certain action.
   persuasion

9. A promotional activity that encourages customers to participate rather than just observe.
   event marketing

10. The unique address of a document, web page, or website on the Internet.
    uniform resource locator (URL)

11. A software application developed for use by mobile devices.
    mobile app

12. A meeting set by a business or organization for which the media is invited to attend.
    press conference

13. Involves using promotions to make customers actively seek out the product.
    pull promotional concept

14. Combines all forms of marketing communication in a coordinated way.
    integrated marketing communications (IMC)

15. A story featuring useful company information written by the company PR contact.
    press release

16. An advertising message sent through the US Postal Service to current or potential customers.
    direct mail

17. Bar codes that, when scanned with a smartphone, connect the user to a website or other digital information.
    quick response (QR) codes

18. Promoting specific products or services offered by the business.
    product promotion

19. The process of indexing a website to rank it higher on the list when a search is conducted.
    search engine optimization (SEO)

20. The number of copies distributed to subscribers and stores for sale.
    circulation

Chapter 23   Promotions

195

Name _____

True or False

Decide whether each statement is true or false and enter *T* or *F* on the line provided. If the statement is false, rewrite the statement to make it true.

1. Institutional promotion is promoting a product, rather than a specific company.
   False. Institutional promotion is promoting a company, rather than a specific product.

2. The end goal of most promotions is to persuade people to buy a product.   True

3. Messages that remind are those appearing in multiple places over a period of time.   True

4. Most marketing plans include a *multi year* promotional plan.   False. Most marketing plans include a one-year promotional plan.

5. Publicity is any nonpersonal communication paid for by an identified sponsor.   False. Advertising is any nonpersonal communication paid for by an identified sponsor.

6. Preselling is creating interest and demand for a product long after it is available for sale.
   False. Preselling is creating interest and demand for a product before it is available for sale.

7. Infomercials are shorter than commercials.   False. Infomercials are longer than commercials, usually 30 minutes.

8. A manufacture's rebate is a return of a portion of the purchase price of an item.
   True

9. Reactive public relations is when the company presents itself in a positive manner to build an image.
   False. Proactive public relations is when the company presents itself in a positive manner to build an image.

10. Personal selling is any indirect contact between a salesperson and a customer.   False. Personal selling is any direct contact between a salesperson and a customer.

Copyright Goodheart-Willcox Co., Inc.

Part 2: Marketing by the Numbers

Viral Marketing and Exponential Growth

Viral marketing, also called *buzz marketing*, is information about products or companies that customers or viewers are compelled to pass along to others. E-mail is a popular medium for sending promotional messages marketers hope will *go viral*, or be forwarded by many people. For example, an e-mail service provider attaches a promotional message to the bottom of each e-mail. Every time a subscriber sends an e-mail message, he or she also sends a promotional message for the service.

Viral marketing is popular because the number of messages sent can grow exponentially. What is exponential growth? *Exponential growth* occurs when the increase in a quantity occurs by multiplication, rather than addition. Growth by addition, or finding a sum total, is called *arithmetic growth*. In the following example, arithmetic growth occurs when 2 new customers are added every day. Exponential growth occurs when the number of customers doubles, or is multiplied by 2, every day. By the sixth day, the company that has added two new customers a day has only 11 customers. But the company that multiplied its customers by 2 every day has 32 customers—21 more customers than the first company. The concept is shown in the following table.

	Arithmetic vs. Exponential Growth					
	Day 1	Day 2	Day 3	Day 4	Day 5	Day 6
Arithmetic (Added 2)	1	3	5	7	9	11
Exponential (Multiplied by 2)	1	2	4	8	16	32

Suppose you get an interesting e-mail a message you want others to see. Perhaps you send the e-mail to two people. Then, those two people send that e-mail to two more people, and so on. This is how messages become viral. This situation is similar to the number of customers doubling every day. See the following diagram.

Exponential Growth by Doubling

$2^0 = 1$	X
$2^1 = 2$	X X
$2^2 = 4$	XX XX
$2^3 = 8$	XX XX XX XX
$2^4 = 16$	XX XX XX XX XX XX XX XX
$2^5 = 32$	XX XX XX XX XX XX XX XX XX XX XX XX XX XX XX XX

This form of growth is called exponential because it can be described by a mathematical expression called an *exponent*. Another term for an exponent is *power*. An exponent is a number indicating how many times another number is multiplied by itself. The number being multiplied is called the *base number*. An exponent is written as a superscript next to the base. For example, 2^3 means the number 2 is multiplied by itself three times: $2 \times 2 \times 2 = 8$. It is read as "2 to the third power." The number 2 is the base, and the number 3 is the exponent. Any number raised to the zero (0) power is defined as one (1). Thus, $2^0 = 1$. Any number raised to the first power (1) is defined as the number itself. Thus, $2^1 = 2$.

Chapter 23   Promotions

Name _____

Now, take a look at exponential growth through tripling. Imagine that each person who gets that e-mail sends it to three people, and so on. In this case, the base number is three. Fill in the following chart to show exponential growth by tripling.

$3^0 = 1$	X
$3^1 = 3$	X X X
$3^2 = 9$	XXX XXX XXX
$3^3 = 27$	XXX XXX XXX XXX XXX XXX XXX XXX XXX
$3^4 = 81$	XXX XXX XXX XXX XXX XXX XXX XXX XXX XXX XXX XXX XXX XXX XXX XXX XXX XXX XXX XXX XXX XXX XXX XXX XXX XXX XXX

Copyright Goodheart-Willcox Co., Inc.

Part 3: Demonstrate Your Knowledge

Push and Pull Promotional Strategies

A push promotional strategy involves taking the product to the customers. A pull promotional strategy involves using promotions to make customers actively seek out the product. Read each scenario and answer the questions using complete sentences.

New Skiers

The first ski resort recently opened in China. Skiing had been practically unknown in China before the new resort opened. The resort developers promoted skiing as a fun family activity while emphasizing the importance of families spending time together.

One family said, "Skiing is a nice change from going shopping." The new skiers layered on their warmest clothes and rented skis from the resort. Due to the newness of the sport, sleek skiing outfits and professional-quality ski equipment are not yet in demand.

1. Which promotional strategy (push or pull) would you recommend to manufacturers of ski clothing and equipment that want to promote their products in China? Explain your answer.

   Student answers will vary.

Sports in Uniform

Challenging sports, such as rock climbing and white-water kayaking, appeal to a relatively small number of people. Among those few are members of the military. Often when soldiers found the rugged, high-tech clothing and equipment they needed, they would tell others about it. In the mountains of North Carolina, there were a few tiny companies making this gear. The output of those companies was small because product demand was low. When branches of the military needed better equipment, the members who knew about those companies recommended the outdoor-gear industry. Once the military placed its orders, dozens of new factories sprang up to increase production.

2. Which promotional strategy, push or pull, was operating here? Explain your answer.

   Student answers will vary.

Pass the Mustard

Today's supermarkets have entire sections for different mustards. However, thirty years ago, *mustard* meant French's yellow mustard. Then, the makers of Grey Poupon mustard began running a clever media campaign. In the TV ad, an elegant man sitting in a Rolls Royce, holding a silver platter of beef, nods to his chauffeur. The chauffeur reaches into the glove compartment and brings out the Grey Poupon. Another Rolls Royce pulls up. A man leans out and asks, "Pardon me. Would you have any Grey Poupon?" The mustard is handed over with a smile. The commercial ends with a voice-over, "One of life's finer pleasures."

By the late 1980s, Grey Poupon sales had overtaken French's yellow mustard.

3. How did Grey Poupon position itself? With, above, or against French's? How did the commercial make this clear?

   Student answers will vary.

Chapter 23   Promotions

Name _____

Electronic Promotion

Home Buying on the Internet

Shopping for a house is a time-consuming process. Real estate agents take prospective buyers from one house to another. Now, many real estate agencies are using the Internet to promote their listings by creating websites with information about houses for sale. Prospective home buyers can see photos of each house plus a detailed list of features. Some websites offer maps so buyers can find where a house is located. Some offer virtual tours of houses, so buyers can see each room and even views from the windows.

1. How have these websites changed the way buyers shop for houses?
   Student answers will vary.

2. How have these websites benefited the real estate agents?
   Student answers will vary.

3. Do you think people will start buying houses directly from the Internet, without actually visiting the house? Explain your answer.
   Student answers will vary.

Backyard Birds: Online and Off

Backyard Birds sells birdhouses, feeders, baths, seed, binoculars, and other items for bird lovers. For 35 years, it sent out thousands of catalogs every year through the mail. With the popularity of the Internet, Backyard Birds put its catalog on its website. Instead of mailing the annual catalog, customers received postcards with the company's web address. Two years later, it discontinued its online catalog and went back to mailing a printed catalog.

1. Why do you think Backyard Birds created a website?
   Student answers will vary.

2. Why do you think the website failed as a sales tool?
   Student answers will vary.

3. Do you think it was a good idea for Backyard Birds to discontinue the online catalog? Explain your answer.
   Student answers will vary.

4. Imagine Backyard Birds has hired you to help them improve sales. What would you recommend? Explain your answer.
   Student answers will vary.

Part 4: Be Your Own Leader

Talk to a Leader

Identify a leader in your community whom you admire. This person could be a family member, your employer, a teacher or coach at school, or someone else you admire. Have your teacher approve the person you wish to interview. Contact the leader to set up an interview. The preferred contact method would be in person; however, you may choose to call or e-mail the person.

Use the following interview questions and add a minimum of two questions of your own. Have your instructor approve your questions. Take notes during the interview. Once the interview is completed, key a one- or two-page summary. Be prepared to share your findings with the rest of the class.

1. How would you describe your leadership style?
   Student answers will vary.

2. What does leadership mean to you?
   Student answers will vary.

3. Who has been the greatest influence on you as a leader?
   Student answers will vary.

4. As a future leader, what should I be doing now to improve my leadership skills?
   Student answers will vary.

5. What advice would you give me as a future leader?
   Student answers will vary.

6. How important is networking to a leader? What do you do to network with others?
   Student answers will vary.

Chapter 23   Promotions

Name _____

7. What do you do to inspire others?
   Student answers will vary.

8. How would others describe you?
   Student answers will vary.

9. Your Question: Student answers will vary.

10. Your Question: Student answers will vary.

Name _____ Date _____ Period _____

CHAPTER 24 Advertising

Part 1: Check Your Knowledge

Matching

Write the correct term for each definition on the line provided.

Key Terms

action word
advertising agency
advertising campaign
Advertising Self-Regulatory Council (ASRC)
art
copy
creative plan
frequency
headline
hook

layout
lead time
posttesting
pretesting
reach
signature
typography
typeface
weight
white space

1. Ad text that provides information and sells the product.
   copy

2. Identifies the person or company paying for the ad.
   signature

3. In typography, it refers to the thickness and slant of the letters.
   weight

4. The words designed to grab attention so viewers will read the rest of the ad.
   headline

5. Measures the effectiveness of an ad before it is seen by the general public.
   pretesting

6. A coordinated series of linked ads with a single idea or theme.
   advertising campaign

Copyright Goodheart-Willcox Co., Inc.

203

7. The number of viewers expected to see an ad.
   reach

8. A firm that creates ads, commercials, and other parts of promotional campaigns for its clients.
   advertising agency

9. The aspect of an ad that grabs attention.
   hook

10. A particular style for the printed letters of the alphabet, punctuation, and numbers.
    typeface

11. The blank areas on a page where there is no art or copy.
    white space

12. Establishes the policies and procedures for advertising self-regulation.
    Advertising Self-Regulatory Council (ASRC)

13. The visual aspect of the words printed on a page; it includes decisions about typeface, size and weight.
    typography

14. The number of times the ad appears before the same customer.
    frequency

15. The time between reserving the ad space and when it actually runs for an ad.
    lead time

16. Measures changes in brand awareness or attitude toward the brand after a campaign.
    posttesting

17. A verb telling the readers what to do.
    action word

18. Outlines the goals, primary message, budget, and target market for different ad campaigns.
    creative plan

19. The arrangement of the headline, copy, and art on a page.
    layout

20. All of the elements that illustrate the message of an ad.
    art

Chapter 24 Advertising

205

Name _____

True or False

Decide whether each statement is true or false and enter *T* or *F* on the line provided. If the statement is false, rewrite the statement to make it true.

1. Advertising can change beliefs and attitudes about products and help people make buying decisions. True

2. The more often a person sees an ad, the better the chance the message will be remembered. True

3. Not every advertising campaign has a goal of increased product sales. True

4. Customer-retention metrics measure overall customer satisfaction, ease of learning and using a product, and first-time user satisfaction. False. Product metrics measure overall customer satisfaction, ease of learning and using a product, and first-time user satisfaction.

5. Most large companies use an advertising agency. True

6. An account manager chooses the visual graphics and creates the overall design for an ad or commercial. False. A graphic designer chooses the visual graphics and creates the overall design.

7. A general rule recommends that headlines have a maximum of seven words. True

8. Many advertisers think the headline is the most important part of the ad. True

9. The body copy of a print ad attracts attention, while the headline presents the selling message. False. The headline of a print ad attracts attention, while the body copy presents the selling message.

10. The graphics are often the last part of the ad a reader notices. False. The graphics are often the first part of the ad a reader notices.

Copyright Goodheart-Willcox Co., Inc.

Part 2: Marketing by the Numbers

Evaluate an Advertising Campaign

A national restaurant chain decided to develop an advertising campaign for the continental United States. One of the objectives of the campaign was to increase sales by 5%. The following table contains the sales data for each restaurant for the three months before and after the ad campaign ran. Determine the results of the ad campaign for each of the restaurants. Round percents to the nearest tenth. Indicate a decrease by placing the number in parentheses. Indicate if the campaign objective was met for each location by writing *yes* or *no* in the last column. Finally, answer the questions that follow based on your calculations.

Location of Restaurant	Sales Before Campaign ($)	Sales After Campaign ($)	Difference ($)	Percent Change (%)	Objective Met? (Yes or No)
Los Angeles, CA	$445,834	$457,548	$11,714	2.6%	No
Colorado Springs, CO	203,421	225,490	22,069	10.8	Yes
Tampa, FL	325,624	329,563	3,939	1.2	No
Atlanta, GA	175,438	173,435	2,003	1.1	No
Chicago, IL	205,325	220,928	15,603	7.6	Yes
Boston, MA	265,539	287,353	21,814	8.2	Yes
Detroit, MI	198,213	205,562	7,349	3.7	No
Nashua, NH	125,392	135,761	10,369	8.3	Yes
Bismarck, ND	98,012	115,394	17,382	17.7	Yes
Cleveland, OH	268,595	280,116	11,521	4.3	No
Portland, OR	156,320	182,848	26,528	17.0	Yes
Pittsburgh, PA	216,865	247,004	30,139	13.9	Yes
Houston, TX	288,225	300,617	12,392	4.3	No
Reston, VA	157,306	189,430	32,124	20.4	Yes
Casper, WY	105,693	117,324	11,631	11.0	Yes

Chapter 24   Advertising

Name _____

Use the information from the chart on the previous page to help you answer the following questions.

1. How many restaurants are in the chain?
   15

2. How many restaurants met the objective of a 5% sales increase?
   9

3. What percentage of the total restaurants met the sales objective?
   60%

4. How close were the restaurants that met the sales objective to the objective?
   Between 2.6% and 15.4% over the objective of 5%

5. How many restaurants did *not* meet the objective?
   6

6. What percentage of the total restaurants did *not* meet the sales objective?
   40%

7. How close were the restaurants that did *not* meet the sales objective to the objective?
   Between 0.7% and 3.8% below the objective of 5%. One lost 1.1% in sales.

8. Is there a correlation between the geographic locations of the restaurants and whether or not the sales objective was met? Explain your answer.
   Student answers will vary.

9. Write an evaluation of the ad campaign.
   Student answers will vary.

10. What recommendations would you make to the chain on the next step(s) to take?
    Student answers will vary.

Newspaper Advertising Rates

Most newspapers sell advertising space by the column inch. A *column inch* is an area of one column wide by one inch long. Newspapers state their advertising rates as a certain amount of money per column inch, such as $30 per column inch. To calculate the cost of any given ad, multiply the column inch rate by the number of columns of the ad. Then, multiply that answer by the number of inches.

(column inch rate × number of columns) × number of inches = cost of ad

For example, one newspaper has a column inch rate of $18. If the size of your ad is three columns wide and four inches long, you would multiply $18 by 3 columns, which equals $54. Next, multiply $54 by 4 inches = $216. The ad would cost $216 to run in that newspaper on one day.

Suppose a region has two newspapers. The *Local Reporter* is located in a small town. Its readership includes the 12 surrounding communities. The *Local Reporter*'s ad rate is $19.50 per column inch. The *City Tribune* is located in the area's largest city and is distributed to a larger audience, including those cities and towns covered by the *Local Reporter*. The *City Tribune*'s ad rate is $24.75 per column inch.

Complete the following table by calculating the cost to place ads of different sizes in each newspaper. The first one is completed for you as an example.

Size of Ad (# of columns)	Size of Ad (in inches)	Cost in Local Reporter ($)	Cost in City Tribune ($)
2	4	$156.00	$198.00
3	3	175.50	222.75
2	8	312.00	396.00
4	3	234.00	297.00
4	5	390.00	495.00

Chapter 24   Advertising   209

Name _____

Part 3: Demonstrate Your Knowledge

Advertising copy for print media is meant to be read, but copy for radio ads is meant to be heard. Radio copy has to be short and clear with simple, easy-to-follow sentences. Read the following print ad. Then create a radio commercial based on the ad.

FORGET THE STOCK MARKET.
SELL YOUR OLD TOYS AND YOU MIGHT MAKE A FORTUNE.
Come to the Yesterplay Appraisal Fair on Saturday, June 8
from 10 a.m.–5 p.m. at the City Convention Center
Do you have your original Barbie doll that is still collecting dust since your Mom bought it in 1959? What about that case of Hot Wheel cars or that G.I. Joe, the one that has been in your basement since you got it for Christmas in 1972?
A mere cleaning of a house can bring hundreds of dollars to someone with the right items, and that's a lot better than you could get at a garage sale.
We can offer the highest prices for mint-condition toys because we often have buyers for the toys before we make the purchases, so there's less risk for us.
Bring as many old toys as you can carry—there is no limit. Appraisals are free.
You are under no obligation to sell your old toys to us,
although once people see how much we will pay for the toys, it is a win/win situation.

Radio Commercial

Turn this print ad into a 30-second radio commercial.

Student answers will vary.

Copyright Goodheart-Willcox Co., Inc.

Part 4: Be Your Own Leader

Leaders Know Their Core Values

What is the most important part of a house? It is not the decorations, the back yard, or even the design. It is the foundation. Without a strong foundation, or core, even the prettiest house in the most beautiful area will begin to crumble. It is the same with leadership. Strong leaders know their core values and are able to explain them. What is a core value? A value is your beliefs and your code of ethics. Your values will guide you when making decisions as leader. Without a value system, you may make inconsistent decisions or not know why you are making certain decisions.

Read the following list of core values. Write a checkmark next to those that match your own value system. Next, add three of your own additional values to the core values list. Then, complete the list that follows. Student answers will vary.

Core Values

Friendship		Recognition		Learning	
Authority		Economic Security		Persuasiveness	
Helping Others		Freedom		Confidence	
Honesty		Truth		Recognition	
Education		Humor		Sharing	
Stability		Camaraderie		Thoroughness	
Environment		Commitment		Teamwork	
Money		Compassion		Sincerity	
Excellence		Determination		Relaxation	
Dependability		Efficiency		Recreation	
Status		Exploration		Punctuality	
Harmony		Risk		Creativity	
Challenge		Happiness		Original Work	
Affection		Intuition			
Working with others		Open-mindedness			
Working Alone		Optimism			

1. Review the previous list of personal core values. Choose the ten that are most important to you, and list them in the order of importance.

    1. Student answers will vary.
    2. _____
    3. _____
    4. _____
    5. _____
    6. _____
    7. _____
    8. _____
    9. _____
    10. _____

Name _____ Date _____ Period _____

CHAPTER 25 Visual Merchandising

Part 1: Check Your Knowledge

Matching

Write the correct term for each definition on the line provided.

Key Terms

analogous colors
balance
color wheel
color scheme
complementary colors
design
display
emphasis
fixture
hue
intensity
marquee

movement
point-of-purchase display (POP)
proportion
props
storefront
store image
store layout
texture
triadic colors
value
visual merchandising

1. Refers to the surface quality of materials.
   texture

2. Refers to the way items are placed around an imaginary centerline.
   balance

3. Draws the attention of the viewer to the most important part of a display.
   emphasis

4. Refers to the lightness or darkness of the color, or how much white or black is mixed with the pure color.
   value

5. An item designed to hold something.
   fixture

Copyright Goodheart-Willcox Co., Inc.   211

6. A visual presentation of merchandise or ideas.
   display

7. Created through the location, design, and décor of a retail business.
   store image

8. The purposeful arrangement of materials to produce a certain effect.
   design

9. A description of color combinations.
   color scheme

10. A standard arrangement of 12 colors in a wheel that shows the relationships among the colors.
    color wheel

11. An overhanging structure containing a signboard located at the entrance to the store. It displays information that can be changed.
    marquee

12. A special display usually found near a cash register or where goods are purchased.
    point-of-purchase display (POP)

13. The process of creating floor plans and displays to attract customer attention and encourage purchases.
    visual merchandising

14. Refers to the brightness or dullness of a color.
    intensity

15. Refers to the size and space relationship of all items in a display to each other and to the whole display.
    proportion

16. Three colors that are equally spaced on the color wheel.
    triadic colors

17. It includes the store sign or logo, marquee, display windows, entrances, outdoor lighting, landscaping, and the building itself.
    storefront

18. Objects used in a display to support the theme or to physically support the merchandise.
    props

19. Refers to the way the design guides viewers' eyes over an item or display.
    movement

20. The pure color itself.
    hue

Chapter 25   Visual Merchandising

Name _____

True or False

Decide whether each statement is true or false and enter *T* or *F* on the line provided. If the statement is false, rewrite the statement to make it true.

1. The design of a business exterior is often part of the promotion decision.   False. The design of a business exterior is often part of the place decision.

2. The storage area is where the merchandise is presented to the customer.   False. The selling area is where the merchandise is presented to the customer.

3. A store layout is a floor plan that shows how the space in a store will be used.   True

4. Display fixtures are often customized to meet the needs of the particular product.   True

5. A point-of-purchase display is designed to increase impulse purchases as customers are waiting to pay for their purchases.   True

6. Motion is often the most dramatic and noticeable design element.   False. Color is often the most dramatic and noticeable design element.

7. The in-fashion colors rarely change.   False. The in-fashion colors change frequently.

8. If an equal amount of a primary and secondary colors are mixed, an intermediate color is created.   True

9. Colors found next to each other on a color wheel are called complementary colors.   False. Colors found opposite to one another on a color wheel are called complementary colors.

10. Analogous colors are opposite to one another on the color wheel.   False. Analogous colors are adjacent to one another on the color wheel.

Copyright Goodheart-Willcox Co., Inc.

Part 2: Marketing by the Numbers

Displays

Imagine you are a marketing consultant planning a display. You want a string of lights around each window in each display. Before you can complete the display, you must determine how many lights you need for the windows. How will you do this?

Perimeter is the distance around the outside of a shape. For shapes consisting of straight lines, you add the length of each line in the shape to get the perimeter. For square shapes, each side is the same length, so you can multiply the length of the one side by four (4). If you were to represent the perimeter of a square as a formula, it would be $P = 4s$, where P stands for perimeter and s stands for side.

In a rectangle, the two opposite sides are the same length. To determine the perimeter of a rectangle, you multiply the length of one side by two (2). Then, you multiply the second side by two (2), and add the previous two results together. If you were to represent the perimeter of a rectangle as a formula, it would be $P = 2l + 2w$, where P stands for perimeter, l stands for length, and w stands for width.

Part 1

Using the information in the chart below, calculate the perimeter for each window.

Window	Length in Feet	Width in Feet	Calculate 2l + 2w	Perimeter in Feet
1	6 ft.	4 ft.	(2 × 6) + (2 × 4)	20 ft.
2	8	4	(2 × 8) + (2 × 4)	24
3	8	12	(2 × 8) + (2 × 12)	40
4	8	15	(2 × 8) + (2 × 15)	46
5	24	36	(2 × 24) + (2 × 36)	120

Part 2

Light strings are available as follows:
- 25 ft. for $9.95;
- 50 ft. for $18.95; and
- 100 ft. for $29.95.

Decide the combination of strands you need and how much they will cost. Show your calculations.

3 of the 25 ft. strands, or 3 X $9.95 = $29.85;

2 of the 50 ft. strands, or 2 X $19.95 = $37.90;

1 of the 100 ft. strands, or $29.95 for a total of $97.70

Chapter 25   Visual Merchandising   **215**

Name _____

Part 3: Demonstrate Your Knowledge

Store Layout

Imagine that you are a marketing consultant who was hired to assist in the design of a new store. Your first project is to design the store layout. Answer the following questions.

1. Select a type of store for which you are designing a layout. Possibilities include a bookstore, car dealership, clothing store, craft store, jewelry store, shoe store, or sports equipment store, etc. Write the type of store.
   Student answers will vary.

2. List the kinds of merchandise the store will carry.
   Student answers will vary.

3. What kind of fixtures would be needed to display that merchandise?
   Student answers will vary.

4. Indicate how customers will move through your store.
   Student answers will vary.

5. Sketch your layout in the box provided. Be sure to include the following items in your layout:
   - sales area (fixtures, merchandise, counters, cash registers, props, lighting) and
   - sales support areas (customer amenities, staff areas, and merchandise receiving and storage).

Student answers will vary.

Part 4: Be Your Own Leader

Leaders Create a Positive Atmosphere

Leaders influence group members through their values and beliefs. A strong leader creates an atmosphere in which the members are willing and excited to complete their work. In the previous chapter, you identified your core values. Choose the one value that best describes you, and then create a banner to reflect this value. If you did not complete the leadership exercise in Chapter 24, refer to the list of core values, and choose the one that best describes you.

1. Identify your value.
   Student answers will vary.

2. Using the dictionary, write the definition of the word.
   Student answers will vary.

3. Develop your own definition of the word.
   Student answers will vary.

4. Find three quotes that either include the word or help to explain your value.
   a. *Student answers will vary.*
   b. _____
   c. _____

5. Find at least three other ways to show the meaning of the value. For example, what does the value look like in action? Draw a picture, write a testimonial, or find another creative way to define or show the value in action. Use a separate sheet of paper if needed.

   Student answers will vary.

6. Using the information from the previous five questions, create a personal banner to reflect your value.

   _____'S PERSONAL BANNER

   Student answers will vary.

Name _____ Date _____ Period _____

CHAPTER 26
Personal Selling

Part 1: Check Your Knowledge

Matching
Write the correct term for each definition on the line provided.

Key Terms

approach
business-to-business (B2B) selling
business-to-consumer (B2C) selling
buying signal
call center
close
cold calling
customer service
customer-service mindset
customer support team
excuse
feature-benefit selling
greeting approach
lead
merchandise approach
objection
overselling
preapproach
quality service
relationship selling
service approach
substitute selling
suggestion selling
telemarketing

1. The moment when a customer agrees to buy a product.
   close

2. The technique of showing products that are different from the originally requested product, but will still fit the customer need.
   substitute selling

3. The step in which the salesperson makes the first in-person contact with a potential customer.
   approach

4. The method of showing the major selling features of a product and how it benefits the customer.
   feature-benefit selling

5. The employees who take orders or answer questions coming into the company via phone or website.
   customer support team

Copyright Goodheart-Willcox Co., Inc.   217

6. Focuses on building long-term relationships with customers.
   relationship selling

7. The process of selling from one business to another business.
   business-to-business (B2B) selling

8. A potential customer.
   lead

9. Consists of tasks performed before contact is made with a customer.
   preapproach

10. The attitude that customer satisfaction always comes first.
    customer-service mindset

11. Consists of a friendly welcome to the store or department.
    greeting approach

12. A personal reason not to buy.
    excuse

13. The technique of suggesting additional items to go with merchandise requested by a customer.
    suggestion selling

14. Meets customer needs as well as the standards for customer service set by the company.
    quality service

15. Starts with the phrase, "May I help you?"
    service approach

16. The process of selling to consumers.
    business-to-consumer (B2C) selling

17. An office that is set up for the purpose of receiving and making customer calls for an organization.
    call center

18. The way in which a business provides services before, during, and after a purchase.
    customer service

19. A verbal or nonverbal sign that a customer is ready to purchase.
    buying signal

20. A conversation that starts with a comment about the product.
    merchandise approach

Chapter 26 Personal Selling

Name _____

True or False

Decide whether each statement is true or false and enter T or F on the line provided. If the statement is false, rewrite the statement to make it true.

1. By meeting customer needs with a product or service, a company can grow its sales.
   True

2. Telemarketing is nonpersonal selling done over the telephone. False. Telemarketing is personal selling done over the telephone.

3. People like personal contact when making a buying decision. True

4. Cold calling is the process of making contact with people who are expecting a sales contact.
   False. Cold calling is the process of making contact with people who are not expecting a sales contact.

5. The Internet can be used for personal selling. True

6. Identifying sales leads is used most often in B2C sales. False. Identifying sales leads is used most often in B2B sales.

7. An objection is a concern or other reason a customer has for *not* making a purchase.
   True

8. The contingent close provides the customer with choices between two or three different products. False. The choice close provides the customer with choices between two or three different products.

9. Underselling is promising more than the product or the business can deliver. False. Overselling is promising more than the product or the business can deliver.

10. Company image is often projected through employee performance. True

Part 2: Marketing by the Numbers

Selling on Commission

Many sales careers offer a commission as a means of compensation. *Commission* is payment based on a percentage of sales. Real estate agents, car salespersons, and insurance agents are often paid on commission.

There are two types of jobs that are paid on commission. *Straight commission* is a job for which the commission is the only pay that the person earns. The other type is *commission with base pay*. With this type of compensation, the person earns a salary or hourly wage plus commission on sales made.

Real estate agents are usually paid on straight commission. The typical commission for a real estate agent is between 2 and 6 percent. The following chart shows the selling prices of several houses plus several different rates of commission that an agent might earn. Complete the chart by calculating the commission for each property at each commission rate.

Property Selling Price	Real Estate Commissions in Dollars				
	2% Commission	3% Commission	4% Commission	5% Commission	6% Commission
$50,000	$1,000	$1,500	$2,000	$2,500	$3,000
75,000	1,500	2,250	3,000	3,750	4,500
150,000	3,000	4,500	6,000	7,500	9,000
200,000	4,000	6,000	8,000	10,000	12,000
250,000	5,000	7,500	10,000	12,500	15,000
299,000	5,980	8,970	11,960	14,950	17,940
314,500	6,290	9,435	12,580	15,725	18,870
379,000	7,580	11,370	15,160	18,950	22,740
399,000	7,980	11,970	15,960	19,950	23,940
450,000	9,000	13,500	18,000	22,500	27,000

Chapter 26 Personal Selling 221

Name _____

Part 3: Demonstrate Your Knowledge

Observing Potential Customers

Read the following five scenarios from a busy shopping mall. For each scene, answer these questions:
A. What do you think is happening based on your observation?
B. If you were the salesperson, what would you say or do in this situation?

Ibbotson's Clothing for Men and Women

1. A young woman chats on her cell phone as she strolls through the Cruise Wear department. She idly sorts through the clothing racks, occasionally holding up an item, all the while laughing and talking.

    A. What do you think is going on, based on your observation?
    Student answers will vary.

    B. If you were the salesperson, what would you say or do in this situation?
    Student answers will vary.

2. A middle-age woman briskly walks in the store followed by a slower-moving man of similar age. When they reach the Special Occasion Dresses department, he sits down heavily in a chair and sighs as she starts looking through the dresses.

    A. What do you think is going on, based on your observation?
    Student answers will vary.

    B. If you were the salesperson, what would you say or do in this situation?
    Student answers will vary.

Wallace and Son, Giftware Department

3. A woman in her thirties pushes two small children in a stroller. She looks at crystal vases, silver bowls, and candlesticks. She moves quickly, but sometimes stops to check a price.

    A. What do you think is going on, based on your observation?
    Student answers will vary.

    B. If you were the salesperson, what would you say or do in this situation?
    Student answers will vary.

Copyright Goodheart-Willcox Co., Inc.

World Travel Luggage, Inc.

4. An elderly man walks wearily but directly to the area where the suitcases are displayed. He looks at the suitcases for a while, reading the tags and lifting the pieces. Then he stands there, looking over each piece of luggage.

    A. What do you think is going on, based on your observation?
    Student answers will vary.

    B. If you were the salesperson, what would you say or do in this situation?
    Student answers will vary.

5. Four teen boys are examining the high-end sports equipment bags. You are about to go over to assist them. Then, you realize there is something different about their method of communication using hand gestures and facial expressions. They do not seem like typical American teenagers.

    A. What do you think is going on, based on your observation?
    Student answers will vary.

    B. If you were the salesperson, what would you say or do in this situation?
    Student answers will vary.

Chapter 26 Personal Selling 223

Name _____

Part 4: Be Your Own Leader

Leaders Learn from Others

Find and read two articles on leadership written by a leader. The articles should be a minimum of one page each. Print a copy of the articles to attach to this worksheet. Write a summary of the articles in the space provided. Your summary should be at least two paragraphs in length and use complete sentences. Use at least two quotes from the articles in your summary. Make sure to use quotation marks to identify when you are quoting. After writing the summary, write your Key Takeaways, or the most important things you learned. Then, answer the questions that follow.

Title of Article 1: Student answers will vary.

Author: Student answers will vary.

Source/Date: Student answers will vary.

Summary:

Student answers will vary.

_____

_____

_____

_____

_____

Key Takeaways (at least two):

Student answers will vary.

_____

_____

_____

_____

Copyright Goodheart-Willcox Co., Inc.

Title of Article 2: _Student answers will vary._

Author: _Student answers will vary._

Source/Date: _Student answers will vary._

Summary:
Student answers will vary.

Key Takeaways (at least two):
Student answers will vary.

1. What are the similarities in the two articles?
   Student answers will vary.

2. What are the differences between the two articles?
   Student answers will vary.

3. Did you disagree with any points in the article? If yes, identify the points and explain why you disagree. If not, explain why you agree with the writer's points.
   Student answers will vary.

Name _____ Date _____ Period _____

CHAPTER 27
Management Skills

Part 1: Check Your Knowledge

Matching

Write the correct term for each definition on the line provided.

Key Terms

adaptability
agenda
attitude
collaboration
conflict
diversity
empathy
ergonomics
give notice
initiative
interpersonal skill
leader
leadership
motion
multitasking
optimism
parliamentary procedure
procrastination
role
self-motivation
stereotyping
team
work habit

1. A recommendation for action to be taken by the group.
   motion

2. Working with others to achieve a common goal.
   collaboration

3. Consists of two or more people working together to achieve a common goal.
   team

4. Performing several tasks at the same time.
   multitasking

5. The inner urge to achieve set goals.
   self-motivation

Copyright Goodheart-Willcox Co., Inc.   225

6. Having people who are different races or who have different cultures in a group or organization.
   diversity

7. The expectation that things will turn out well.
   optimism

8. The science of adapting the workstation to fit the needs of the worker and lessen injury.
   ergonomics

9. A person who guides others to a goal.
   leader

10. A process for holding a meeting so that the meeting is orderly and democratic.
    parliamentary procedure

11. The part that someone has in a family, society, or other group.
    role

12. A situation in which disagreements lead to hostile behavior, such as shouting or fighting.
    conflict

13. The ability to make changes to be a better match, or fit, in new situations.
    adaptability

14. A skill that enables a person to interact with others in a positive way.
    interpersonal skill

15. Classifying or generalizing about a group of people with a given set of characteristics.
    stereotyping

16. The way a person looks at the world and responds to events.
    attitude

17. The personal energy and desire that is needed to do something.
    initiative

18. A basic, routine action carried out every day at work.
    work habit

19. The ability of a person to guide others to a goal.
    leadership

20. The list of topics to be discussed, decisions to be made, or other goals for a meeting.
    agenda

Chapter 27 Management Skills

Name _____

True or False

Decide whether each statement is true or false and enter *T* or *F* on the line provided. If the statement is false, rewrite the statement to make it true.

1. Respect is especially important when you disagree with someone. True

2. Empathy is the ability to see things only from your point of view. False. Empathy is the ability to see things from the point of view of another person.

3. A sense of humor is the ability to see the funny side of things, including making fun of others. False. A sense of humor is the ability to see the funny side of things. It does *not* include making fun of others.

4. Procrastination is doing something now that should be done later. False. Procrastination is the delay of doing something that should be done now.

5. Good health is *not* automatic. True

6. Some people are natural leaders, but most people can develop the traits that make a leader successful. True

7. Disagreements can be useful. True

8. In order to move ahead, you never have to change jobs. False. In order to move ahead, you may have to change jobs on occasion.

9. Giving notice means notifying a coworker of the intention to leave a job. False. Giving notice means notifying a supervisor of the intention to leave a job.

10. One of the keys to success in life is balancing multiple roles. True

Copyright Goodheart-Willcox Co., Inc.

Part 2: Marketing by the Numbers

Fitness Program

As a manager, you are concerned about the overall level of fitness of your 210 employees. You wonder if it would be beneficial to enroll them in a new fitness program at a local gym. Therefore, you hire a consultant to collect data on the fitness levels of your employees in three areas: physical fitness, body mass index, and diet. Calculate and fill in the missing percentages in the following charts. Round to the nearest whole percent. Total percents may not always equal 100 due to rounding.

Physical Fitness

Level of Achievement on a Fitness Test (scale 0 to 100)	Employees (number)	Employees (%)
85 or better	2	1
50 to 85	24	11
Below 50	184	88
Totals	210	100%

Body Mass Index

Body Mass Index	Women (number)	Women (%)	Men (number)	Men (%)
Under 18.5 (Underweight)	22	21	18	17
18.5 – 24.9 (Normal)	44	42	64	62
25 – 29.9 (Overweight)	27	25	13	13
30 and Over (Obese)	13	12	9	9
Totals	106	100%	104	101%

Quality of Diet

Poor Diet Indicators (per day)	Women (number)	Women (%)	Men (number)	Men (%)
Eats fewer than 2,000 calories	22	21%	23	22%
Eats more than 30% fat	17	16	24	23
Eats more than 10% protein	25	24	25	24
Eats fewer than 50% carbohydrates	9	8	8	8
Eats one or less servings of fruit	11	10	16	15
Eats one or less servings of vegetables	13	12	20	19
Total keeping food diaries for this analysis	28	—	35	—

Chapter 27   Management Skills

Name _____

Part 3: Demonstrate Your Knowledge

Section A

Here are three key components of optimism:
- Expect to succeed.
- Do not assume that one failure means everything will fail.
- Do not be quick to blame yourself; the fault may lie elsewhere.

Each of the following situations shows an example of one of the key components of optimism. After reading each situation, write the component being illustrated. Then, explain how the example illustrates the component using complete sentences.

1. Jayden wanted to be a professional marketer, and he had his heart set on the Marketing program at Bentley University. Bentley did not admit Jayden into the school. Assuming he was a failure, Jayden refused to apply elsewhere and became a truck driver. Devin also did not get into Bentley. However, he went to the nearby state school and is now a marketing manager.

   Component of Optimism: <u>Do not assume that one failure means everything will fail.</u>

   Explanation: <u>Student answers will vary.</u>

2. Tracy and Kayla were a special work project team. For months, Tracy had said what a good team they made. Then, Tracy told Kayla that her work was making them both look bad and that Kayla should quit. Kayla felt awful until she heard that Tracy had also told her previous work partner the same thing.

   Component of Optimism: <u>Do not be quick to blame yourself; the fault may lie elsewhere.</u>

   Explanation: <u>Student answers will vary.</u>

3. Alicia was one of 35 applicants asked to interview for a job. She had excellent qualifications, but she kept thinking about how much better the other applicants might be. Although she really wanted the job and felt it was perfect for her, she felt her chances were poor. At her interview, Alicia was very nervous and acted shy and ill at ease. She did not get the job. Tyler had the same qualifications as Alicia. However, at his interview, he was confident and friendly. He had researched the company and asked good questions. He expressed enthusiasm and eagerness to learn. Tyler got the job.

   Component of Optimism: <u>Expect to succeed.</u>

   Explanation: <u>Student answers will vary.</u>

Section B

The attitude of team members can greatly affect team productivity. Read the following situation and answer the questions using complete sentences.

Just in Time?

A company that specializes in building sailboats won a large contract. Part of the contract stated that finished boats had to be delivered by a specific date. The production planning team fell behind schedule because they had to find a new source of materials. The team continues to fall behind schedule but is now making steady progress.

One of the team members, Madeleine, says, "I do not know why we bother rushing. You know we can't make the deadline. The company will lose the contract, and we will be blamed and lose our jobs."

Another team member, Julio, says, "We can make it. We completed more yesterday than expected, and we can do even better today. If we keep up this pace and remain focused, we will make the deadline."

1. How do you think Madeleine's comments made the rest of the team feel?
   Student answers will vary.

2. How might Madeleine's attitude affect the team?
   Student answers will vary.

3. How do you think Julio's comments made the rest of the team feel?
   Student answers will vary.

4. How might Julio's attitude affect the team?
   Student answers will vary.

5. How could the team leader help the team meet the deadline?
   Student answers will vary.

6. Explain why optimism is crucial to a team.
   Student answers will vary.

Chapter 27   Management Skills

Name _____

Part 4: Be Your Own Leader

Interpersonal Skills

In this chapter, you learned about a number of interpersonal skills good leaders should display. Review each of the following interpersonal skills. Check those that you believe represent you. For those you do not check, identify one thing you can do to improve that skill.

Check box	Interpersonal Skill	What I can do to improve this skill. Note: only complete for your unchecked skills.
	Respect	
	Empathetic	
	Open-minded	
	Good sense of humor	
	Trustworthy	
	Dependable	
	Positive attitude	
	Optimistic	
	Self-motivated	
	Initiative	
	Adaptable	
	Good time management	
	Efficient	
	Multitasking	

Copyright Goodheart-Willcox Co., Inc.

Name _____ Date _____ Period _____

CHAPTER 28
Marketing Management

Part 1: Check Your Knowledge

Matching
Write the correct term for each definition on the line provided.

Key Terms

autocratic style
balance sheet
budget
conflict of interest
consulting style
control
cost control
democratic style
emotional intelligence
expense
financial planning
income statement
insider trading
laissez-faire style
net worth
operational planning
organizational chart
plagiarism
proprietary information
revenue
sales forecast
sales-increase factor
staffing
strategic planning
tactical planning

1. Sometimes referred to as trade secrets, this is information a company wishes to keep private.
   proprietary information

2. Using the words of someone else without giving credit to the person who wrote them.
   plagiarism

3. The value of a company.
   net worth

4. Monitoring costs to stay within a planned budget.
   cost control

5. The percentage of expected increase in sales, which is usually a sales goal.
   sales-increase factor

Copyright Goodheart-Willcox Co., Inc. 233

6. The process of setting financial goals and developing methods for reaching them.
   financial planning

7. Management style in which the leader allows employees to make their own decisions about how to complete tasks.
   laissez-faire

8. When an employee uses private company information to purchase company stock or other securities for personal gain.
   insider trading

9. The process of hiring people and matching them to the best positions for their talents.
   staffing

10. The process of determining the short-term goals for the company.
    tactical planning

11. The ability to recognize your emotions, realize how your emotions affect other people, and understand what those emotions mean.
    emotional intelligence

12. A diagram of employee positions showing how the positions interact within the chain of command.
    organizational chart

13. Management style in which the leader makes all decisions without input from others.
    autocratic

14. The money a business takes in for the products or services it sells.
    revenue

15. A financial report showing the net worth of a company.
    balance sheet

16. A prediction of future sales based on past sales and a market analysis for a specific time period.
    sales forecast

17. The process of determining the long-term goals for the company.
    strategic planning

18. Monitor the progress of the team to meet its goals.
    control

19. The process of determining the day-to-day goals for the company.
    operational planning

20. Money that goes out of a business to pay for the items or services it buys.
    expense

Chapter 28   Marketing Management

Name _____

21. A financial report that shows the revenue and expenses for a business during a specific period of time.

income statement

22. A financial plan that reflects anticipated revenue and shows how it will be allocated in the operation of the business.

budget

23. Style of management that is a combination of the democratic and autocratic styles; the manager makes the final decision, but only after considering input from the employees.

consulting

24. Exists when an employee has competing interests or loyalties.

conflict of interest

25. Management style in which the leader encourages team members to participate and share ideas equally.

democratic

True or False

Decide whether each statement is true or false and enter *T* or *F* on the line provided. If the statement is false, rewrite the statement to make it true.

1. Among the many skills a marketer needs are good management skills. **True**

2. The chain of command is the structure in a company including only the highest levels of authority. **False. The chain of command is the structure in a company from the highest to the lowest levels of authority.**

3. The human resources department helps to determine the human resources needs for a department or company. **True**

4. Successful managers recognize the work of others and reward positive performance.
True

5. The employee evaluation process falls under the controlling function of management.
True

6. A confidentiality agreement typically states that the employee will share company information with outsiders. **False. A confidentiality agreement typically states that the employee will not share any company information with outsiders.**

7. Some conflicts of interest are unethical but still legal. **True**

8. Sales forecasts may be qualitative, that is, based on facts and figures. **False. Sales forecasts may be quantitative, that is, based on facts and figures.**

9. By reviewing accounts payable, a marketing manager can determine how much customers still owe to the business. **False. By reviewing accounts receivable, a marketing manager can determine how much customers still owe to the business.**

10. In accounting, a loss is indicated by placing the number in parentheses. **True**

Chapter 28 Marketing Management

Name _____

Part 2: Marketing by the Numbers

Balance Sheet

A *balance sheet* shows a company's net worth on a specific day. A balance sheet uses the record of the company's assets and liabilities to calculate the value, or net worth, of the company. A balance sheet is based on the following equation:

Assets = Liabilities + Owner's Equity

Assets and liabilities for two companies are shown in the following tables. For each company that follows, organize the data into a balance sheet, using the balance sheet provided.

XYZ Company: cash $634; accounts receivable $4,863; inventory $8,297; equipment $6,105; supplies $842; accounts payable $2,623; loan $10,000.

Balance Sheet
XYZ Company
December 31, 20--

ASSETS

Cash	634
Accounts Receivable	4,863
Inventory	8,297
Equipment	6,105
Supplies	842

Total Assets — $20,741

LIABILITIES

Accounts Payable	2,623
Loan Payable	10,000

Total Liabilities — 12,623

OWNERS EQUITY 8,118 — 8,118

Total Liabilities and Owner's Equity — 20,741

DEF Company: cash $1,241; accounts receivable $3,428; inventory $10,792; equipment $9,746; supplies $8,108; accounts payable $7,668; loan $6,000.

Balance Sheet
DEF Company
December 31, 20--

ASSETS

Cash	1,241
Accounts Receivable	3,428
Inventory	10,792
Equipment	9,746
Supplies	8,108
Total Assets	$33,315

LIABILITIES

Accounts Payable	7,668
Loan	6,000
Total Liabilities	13,668

OWNERS EQUITY — 19,647

Total Liabilities and Owner's Equity — 33,315

Chapter 28　Marketing Management

Name _____

Part 3: Demonstrate Your Knowledge

Starting a New Business

The following true story has five underlined phrases. Each phrase is an example of an accounting term. Read the story. Next to each term below, write the number of the underlined phrase that is related to the matching accounting term.

__3__ accounts payable

__2__ accounts receivable

__1__ asset

__4__ liability

__5__ net worth

 Benito P. loves fine food. He had always run a restaurant, but now wanted a less-stressful business. So, he decided to start a fine-foods shop. He would call it the *Ultimate Taste*. It would carry cheeses, mustards, coffees, wines, and candy that people could not find anywhere else. He also planned to offer gourmet takeout, such as salads, pastries, made-to-order sandwiches, and a special daily hot dish. Benito put his ideas into a business plan and took it to a bank.

 The bank agreed to finance the plan. With (1) this money and cash from his savings, Benito bought a store in a resort city and a delivery van. He renovated the store with rich woods and soft lighting and installed a large kitchen. Then, he hired employees: an expert chef and several young people who were eager to learn.

 When the first *Ultimate Taste* opened, it charged twice as much as its competitors. Vacationers and locals alike flocked to the shop, anyway. In the beginning, the higher prices covered the cost of the fresh foods and packaged products. Soon, sales also covered employee wages, utilities, and taxes. After just a year, both bank and owner were pleased with the store's income.

 Benito had seen restaurants go into debt and fail, so he was very careful. He required immediate payment in cash because he did not want (2) customers or other businesses owing money to *Ultimate Taste*. He paid bills promptly because he did not want to (3) owe money to other businesses. The (4) only money he owed was to the bank.

 When Benito had paid back most of the loan, including the cost of borrowing the money, he got another loan and opened a second *Ultimate Taste*. The chef at the first store prepared foods for the second store, and a van delivered it fresh every morning.

 Today, Benito P.'s Ultimate Taste business has a total of seven stores and three delivery vans. There is still one central kitchen, with one chef preparing food for all the stores. Benito says this reduces the amount of money his business has to pay for goods and operations. The chain is valued at (5) over twelve million dollars.

Part 4: Leadership

Leadership or Management Styles

Section A

What is a leadership style? A leadership style is how a leader acts in a situation based on their beliefs, values, and previous experiences. Each of us leads in a different way. The leadership style of a manager also translates in a typical style of managing others. There are different ways to lead and manage. However, there are more appropriate leadership styles for certain situations.

There are four basic leadership/management styles. They are authoritarian, democratic, consulting, and laissez-faire.

Authoritarian leaders (also known as autocratic) are characterized by the following attributes:
- They lead through power.
- They make all major decisions.
- They seek control and authority.

Democratic (also known as participative) leaders are characterized by the following attributes:
- They share in making decisions.
- They keep staff members informed.
- They participate in group tasks.

Consulting leaders are characterized by the following attributes:
- They combine democratic and autocratic styles.
- They seek input from employees.
- They make the final decisions.

Laissez-faire leaders are characterized by the following attributes:
- They allow staff members to set direction.
- Staff members make decisions.
- Staff members set goals and solve problem.

Chapter 28   Marketing Management

Name _____

In this exercise, you will learn about the various leadership styles and provide an example of a leader or manager you know that demonstrates that leadership style.

Do an Internet search for each leadership/management style to help you identify times when one style is better to use than another. Fill in the following chart by listing one or more times when that leadership style should and should *not* be used. Finally, list one specific example. Use the first row as a reference for how to complete chart. Student answers will vary.

Leadership Style	Should be used when:	Should *not* be used when:	Specific Example
Authoritarian	A quick decision should be made	Project members need to do a lot of problem solving	A manufacturer needs to make changes to department orders immediately to meed a deadline.
Authoritarian (use new examples)			
Democratic			
Consulting			
Laissez-Faire			

Section B

What is your leadership/management style? Take the quiz that follows to determine your dominant style. Read each statement and place a checkmark next to those that best describe you. Do not spend a lot of time thinking about each statement. Go with your first response. Student answers will vary.

1. ____I prefer making my own decisions.

2. ____I like others to make their own decisions.

3. ____I listen to others and seek their input when making decisions.

4. ____I listen to others and seek their input before making the final decision.

5. ____When working on a project, I will provide resources for the group.

6. ____I only want to be responsible for my own decisions.

7. ____I often listen to others before making a decision.

8. ____If a group is going in the wrong direction, I bring the group together to reach consensus on a solution.

9. ____If a group is going in the wrong direction, I will correct them.

10. ____If a group is going in the wrong direction, I will seek member input before making a decision about how to correct the problem.

11. ____I like to vote on major issues so that each person has a voice.

12. ____I prefer that each person in the group decide what he or she wants to do.

13. ____When working with others, I would prefer to make the task assignments to each person.

14. ____In a group, I would prefer that each person is allowed to complete his or her own work assignment without much interference.

15. ____I like to talk with others before I choose the solution to a problem.

16. ____I like to talk with others and have them provide their input in writing or verbally so that we have agreement within the group.

Review the following answer key. For each statement you checked, place an X next to the matching number below. For example, if you checked statement #2 in the list above, put an X next to the number 2 below. Total your Xs for each row to determine your dominant leadership/management style.
Student answers will vary.

___1, ___5, ___9, ___13	Authoritarian	Total number checked	_____
___3, ___8, ___11, ___16	Democratic	Total number checked	_____
___4, ___7, ___10, ___15	Consulting	Total number checked	_____
___2, ___6, ___12, ___14	Laissez-Faire	Total number checked	_____

Chapter 28   Marketing Management

243

Name _____

Review the information you gathered from Section B. Then, answer the following questions.

What is your dominant leadership/management style?

Student answers will vary.

Do you agree with the dominant style indicated by the quiz? Explain your answer.

Student answers will vary.

Situational Leadership

Leaders may have a dominant style of leadership but that style will not work well in every situation. Great leaders are situational leaders—meaning they utilize situational leadership. *Situational leadership* is making decisions based on the situation. There are three things that affect *situational leadership*: the person or people, the situation, and the leader's ability to handle the situation. For example, suppose your dominant style of leadership is democratic. However, it is Friday and you just received a phone call from one of your best customers explaining that your company was 3,000 parts short on a recently shipped order. This is very important to your customer because production at his company will stop on Monday if they do not have the correct parts, and he will have to find a new supplier. At this point, you might be more of an authoritarian leader and require staff to work overtime to get the parts packed and on a truck to your customer for receipt by Monday.

1. Think about your dominant leadership style. Provide two examples where you did *not* use your dominant leadership style. Provide details and an explanation of why you did not.

    Situation 1: Student answers will vary.

    Reason(s): Student answers will vary.

    Situation 2: Student answers will vary.

    Reason(s): Student answers will vary.

Copyright Goodheart-Willcox Co., Inc.

2. Think of a leader you personally know. The leader could be your boss, a teacher, a coach, a club advisor, or another student who acts in a leadership role within your school or in an outside organization. Name the type of leadership style you believe he or she uses most often and give two or three specific examples.

Person's role (i.e., coach, teacher, principal, boss)

Student answers will vary.

Person's leadership style

Student answers will vary.

Example 1: Student answers will vary.

Example 2: Student answers will vary.

Name _____ Date _____ Period _____

Chapter 29: Planning for Success

Part 1: Check Your Knowledge

Matching

Write the correct term for each definition on the line provided.

Key Terms

ability
activities-preference inventory
aptitude
Career and Technical Student Organization (CTSO)
career ladder
career plan
cooperative education program
employment trend
entry-level job
information interview
job shadowing
internship
manager
occupation
self-assessment
self-esteem
work values

1. The term used for a specific career area, such as advertising or sales.
   occupation

2. Prepares students for an occupation through a paid job and classes at school.
   cooperative education program

3. A worker who directs the work of others and makes decisions.
   manager

4. An organization for high school students interested in a career area, such as DECA for marketing students.
   Career and Technical Student Organization (CTSO)

5. The process of learning about yourself.
   self-assessment

Copyright Goodheart-Willcox Co., Inc.

245

6. The list of steps that will enable you to achieve your career goal.
   career plan

7. The direction of change in the number of jobs in a particular career.
   employment trend

8. The first job on a career ladder and requires the least amount of education and experience.
   entry-level job

9. A natural talent or natural ability to do something.
   aptitude

10. The aspects of work that are most important to a person.
    work values

11. A series of jobs organized in order of education and experience requirements.
    career ladder.

12. Following a person while he or she does a job.
    job shadowing

13. The confidence and satisfaction you have in yourself.
    self-esteem

14. Programs that allow students to leave school to work in a career for a set amount of time each day and receive classroom credit; they may be paid or unpaid.
    internship

15. A test to determine which activities a person prefers when given a choice.
    activities-preference inventory

Chapter 29   Planning for Success

247

Name _____

True or False

Decide whether each statement is true or false and enter T or F on the line provided. If the statement is false, rewrite the statement to make it true.

1. Success is a lifelong journey. True

2. The most helpful goals are nonspecific. False. The most helpful goals are specific.

3. Interests are related to the satisfaction you get from a job. False. Rewards are related to the satisfaction you get from a job.

4. An ability is the skill to perform a task. True

5. A data job is one focused on working with objects to build or create things. False. An objects job is one focused on working with objects to build or create things.

6. A career ladder is the work a person does regularly in order to earn money. False. A job is the work a person does regularly in order to earn money.

7. Some entry-level jobs have no education or experience requirements. True

8. Talking to someone to learn about his or her career is called an intake interview. False. Talking to someone to learn about his or her career is called an information interview.

9. Many occupations that are *not* growing still need a large number of people each year. True

10. Professional associations may also be called trade associations. True

Copyright Goodheart-Willcox Co., Inc.

Part 2: Marketing by the Numbers

Interest Rates

Many successful marketers began their careers by obtaining the necessary education and training. However, education and training can be costly. One way to pay for these expenses is to save money in a financial institution, such as a bank or credit union. When you deposit money in a bank, the bank uses your money to make money. It then pays you a fee called *interest* for the use of your money, which is called the *principal*.

Money that you deposit in a bank earns interest based on the following formula:

$$P \text{ (Principal)} \times R \text{ (Rate)} \times T \text{ (Time in years)} = I \text{ (Interest)}$$

Principal is the amount of money you deposit in the bank. Interest is the amount your money earns while in the bank. Rate is the percentage rate at which your principal earns interest. Time is the amount of time in years that your money is in the bank.

Two basic types of interest can be earned: simple and compound. *Simple interest* is calculated just once for the time period. *Compound interest* is calculated more than once and includes previously earned interest in each subsequent calculation.

To compute simple interest, use the formula below and substitute the appropriate amounts. For example, suppose you have $350 in the bank. The interest rate is 4%, and you left the principal there for six months.

$$P = \$350, R = 4\% \ (0.04), \text{ and } T = 6 \text{ months } (0.5 \text{ year})$$

$$P \times R \times T = I$$

$$\$350 \times 0.04 \times 0.5 = \$7.00$$

The interest earned on $350 at 4% interest over six months is $7.00.

Perform the calculations and fill in the following chart. The first one is completed for you as an example.

Principal ($)	Rate (%)	Rate as Decimal Fraction	Time (months)	Time as Decimal Fraction of Year	Interest ($)	Principal Plus Interest ($)
$400	2%	0.02	6	0.5	$4.00	$404.00
375	3	0.03	6	0.5	5.63	380.63
725	4	0.04	6	0.5	14.50	739.50
850	4.5	0.045	6	0.5	19.13	869.13
1,420	2.75	0.0275	6	0.5	19.53	1,439.53
1,362	3	0.03	3	0.25	10.22	1,372.22
1,538	3.5	0.035	3	0.25	13.46	1,551.46
1,850	5	0.05	3	0.25	23.13	1,873.13
2,046	2.5	0.025	3	0.25	12.79	2,058.79
2,486	4	0.04	3	0.25	24.86	2,510.86
2,872	4.25	0.0425	9	0.75	91.55	2,963.55
2,906	3.75	0.0375	9	0.75	81.73	2,987.73
3,304	3.5	0.035	9	0.75	86.73	3,390.73
3,598	4.5	0.045	9	0.75	121.43	3,719.43
3,865	2.75	0.0275	12	1.0	106.29	3,971.29

Copyright Goodheart-Willcox Co., Inc.

Chapter 29 Planning for Success

Name _____

Part 3: Demonstrate Your Knowledge

Academic Skills

Many of the skills needed to be successful in a marketing career are learned in school. The following is a list of subjects commonly taken in high school. Choose five from the list. For each subject you choose, (a) describe what you would learn that would be helpful in a marketing career, and (b) describe what skills you might learn to help you succeed in a career in marketing.

School Subjects

art and design	math	sciences
English	music	social studies
fiction and poetry	psychology	writing
foreign language	public speaking	other _____
history	reading	

1. Subject: *Student answers will vary.* _____

   A. Describe what you would learn that would be helpful in a marketing career.
   Student answers will vary. _____
   _____

   B. Describe what skills you might learn to help you succeed in a career in marketing.
   Student answers will vary. _____
   _____

2. Subject: *Student answers will vary.* _____

   A. Describe what you would learn that would be helpful in a marketing career.
   Student answers will vary. _____
   _____

   B. Describe what skills you might learn to help you succeed in a career in marketing.
   Student answers will vary. _____
   _____

3. Subject: *Student answers will vary.* _____

   A. Describe what you would learn that would be helpful in a marketing career.
   Student answers will vary. _____
   _____

   B. Describe what skills you might learn to help you succeed in a career in marketing.
   Student answers will vary. _____
   _____

Copyright Goodheart-Willcox Co., Inc.

4. Subject: __Student answers will vary.__

   A. Describe what you would learn that would be helpful in a marketing career.
   __Student answers will vary.__
   _____

   B. Describe what skills you might learn to help you succeed in a career in marketing.
   __Student answers will vary.__
   _____

5. Subject: __Student answers will vary.__

   A. Describe what you would learn that would be helpful in a marketing career.
   __Student answers will vary.__
   _____

   B. Describe what skills you might learn to help you succeed in a career in marketing.
   __Student answers will vary.__
   _____

Chapter 29   Planning for Success

Name _____

Part 4: Be Your Own Leader

Leaders Keep Track: Building a Leadership Portfolio, Part 1

As a future leader, you need to keep track of what you are learning. In addition to this course, you may have already had many opportunities to develop your leadership skills. By keeping a record of what you have learned, you will not forget your achievements. In order to maintain a record for future use, it is important to create a portfolio. Over the next three chapters, you will develop a leadership portfolio. You can create your portfolio digitally or in a hard-copy format and keep your pages in a three-ring binder. Either way, make sure you have a backup copy in case anything happens to the original. Once you have created your portfolio, review and update it frequently.

A *Leadership Vitae* will be the first part of your portfolio. *Vitae* is a Latin word for a written description of your relevant experience. For this exercise, it will be a listing of your leadership experience. These experiences may have come from leadership roles in academics, clubs or organizations, sports, work, or other outside activities in which you have participated. Every experience counts, whether you were a leader for as little as an hour or for years.

Start by doing an Internet search for a *sample vitae*. Find a layout that you like. Your vitae should be typed once you choose the format. Use the following worksheet to gather the information before you create a formal *Leadership Vitae*. If you have more experience than space provided, make a copy. Use your vitae to apply to colleges, scholarships, jobs, or to talk with your boss about a promotion.

Clubs/Organizations

Club/organization name: Student answers will vary. _____

Leadership experiences: _____

Workshops attended: _____

Positions held: _____

Activities participated in: _____

Club/organization name: Student answers will vary. _____

Leadership experiences: _____

Workshops attended: _____

Positions held: _____

Activities participated in: _____

Sports

Sports team: Student answers will vary. _____

Leadership roles (i.e., team captain, team manager): _____

Position played: _____

Other leadership opportunities (i.e., organize charity game, etc.): _____

_____

Copyright Goodheart-Willcox Co., Inc.

Sports team: _Student answers will vary._

Leadership roles: (i.e., team captain, team manager): _____

Position played: _____

Other leadership opportunities (i.e., organize charity game, etc.): _____

CTSO

Leadership experiences: _Student answers will vary._

Workshops attended: _____

Positions held: _____

Activities participated in: _____

Competitive events: _____

Leadership experiences: _Student answers will vary._

Workshops attended: _____

Positions held: _____

Activities participated in: _____

Competitive events: _____

Presentations Given – Titles/Location/Dates

This could include major class presentations. An example of an entry might read as follows: *Being Financially Fit*, presentation to fifth-grade students, Beachwood Elementary, April 2014.

Presentation 1: _Student answers will vary._

_____

Presentation 2: _____

_____

Presentation 3: _____

_____

Extracurricular Activities

Leadership experiences: _Student answers will vary._

Workshops attended: _____

Positions held: _____

Activities participated in: _____

_____

Chapter 29 Planning for Success **253**

Name _____

Leadership experiences: *Student answers will vary.* _____

Workshops attended: _____

Positions held: _____

Activities participated in: _____

Other Leadership Activities

Employment *Student answers will vary.* _____

Job title: _____

Responsibilities: _____

Activities participated in: _____

Honors and Awards

Student answers will vary. _____

_____

Other Affiliations/Organizations

Student answers will vary. _____

_____

Name _____ Date _____ Period _____

CHAPTER 30: Preparing for Your Career

Part 1: Check Your Knowledge

Matching

Write the correct term for each definition on the line provided.

Key Terms

certificate programs
continuing professional education
cover message
job application
job lead
letter of inquiry
networking

portfolio
postsecondary
reference
résumé
scannable résumé
tech prep
want ad

1. A written document that lists your qualifications for a job, including education and work experience.
   résumé

2. Document that expresses your interest in working for that company, highlights your job qualifications, and asks about any job openings.
   letter of inquiry

3. A selection of materials that you collect and organize to show your qualifications, skills, and talents.
   portfolio

4. The process of making connections with people in the working world.
   networking

5. Information that leads you to a job opening.
   job lead

6. After high school.
   postsecondary

Copyright Goodheart-Willcox Co., Inc.

255

7. Employer's form with spaces for information about you, your education, and your work experience.
   job application

8. Education for people who have already completed their formal schooling and training.
   continuing professional education

9. A person who is willing to talk with potential employers about your job qualifications and personal qualities.
   reference

10. A written advertisement for a job placed by the company that needs the worker.
    want ad

Chapter 30 Preparing for Your Career **257**

Name _____

True or False

Decide whether each statement is true or false and enter *T* or *F* on the line provided. If the statement is false, rewrite the statement to make it true.

1. Many jobs are available for people without a high school diploma. False. Very few jobs are available for people without a high school diploma

2. Paid or unpaid internships do *not* require a related class in school. True

3. One purpose of a cover message is to request an interview. True

4. Many marketing jobs and most management-level positions require a bachelor degree or higher. True

5. Certificate programs are degree training programs. False. Certificate programs are nondegree training programs.

6. One of the most important things to do while job hunting is to keep track of your job leads. True

7. Many job applications no longer ask for several references. False. Many job applications ask for several references.

8. List your work experiences with the most recent job first. True

9. A scannable résumé is formatted to enhance typographical elements, such as bold, bullets, italics, and indents. False. A scannable résumé is formatted to eliminate typographical elements, such as bold, bullets, italics, and indents.

10. A cover message is a letter or e-mail that accompanies your résumé and expresses your interest in a job. True

Part 2: Marketing by the Numbers

Compound Interest

There are two basic types of interest: simple and compound. As you learned in the previous chapter, simple interest is calculated just once for the time period. The formula follows:

I (Interest) = P (Principal) × R (Rate) × T (Time in years)

Many financial institutions offer their customers compound interest. *Compound interest* is calculated more than once for the time period, and it includes previously earned interest in each subsequent calculation. This may sound complex, but as you follow the example below, it will become clear.

Suppose you deposit $400 in a bank that pays 3 percent interest. The bank compounds interest semiannually, or twice a year. If you leave the money in for a year, interest will be calculated, or compounded, twice. The first interest calculation will be after six months; the second interest calculation will be after one year (or the next six months).

The first interest is calculated in the same way as simple interest, but the time period is for six months—even though the total time period is one year. Use the interest formula as follows:

I = P×R×T

$6.00 = $400 × 0.03 × 0.5

The interest on $400 at 3% for six months is $6.00.

The earned interest for the first six months is added to the principal at that time:

$406.00 = $400 + $6.00

After six months, the new principal is $406.

When the second six months of interest is calculated, it is calculated based on your new, larger principal of $406. You will now earn interest on the $6.00 of interest earned in the previous time period as shown in the following calculation.

I = P×R×T

$6.09 = $406 × 0.03 × 0.5

The interest on $406 at 3 percent for six months is $6.09. Interest for the whole year is $12.09 or ($6.00 + $6.09). If the interest had not been compounded, interest for the year would only be $12.00.

The extra nine cents might not seem like much now. However, over a long period of time, it adds up. Your money grows much faster when the interest is compounded. The fact that you now earn interest on previously earned interest is sometimes called *the miracle of compounding*. Compound interest adds up even faster if the time period of compounding is more frequent. Some banks compound interest as often as monthly or daily.

Use the information above to help you complete the activity on the next page.

Chapter 30   Preparing for Your Career

Name _____

Calculate the interest compounded semiannually on the principals in the chart that follows, using the formula you learned previously:

I (Interest) = P (Principal) × R (Rate) × T (Time in years)

Remember to convert the interest rate percent into a decimal. Use 0.5 when calculating time for the first six months as well as the second six months. For the second six months, calculate the interest based on the new, larger principal. The first one is done for you as an example.

		Interest Compounded Semiannually			
		First Six Months		**Second Six Months**	
Principal ($)	**Interest rate (%)**	**Interest ($)**	**Principal plus Interest ($)**	**Interest ($)**	**Principal plus Interest ($)**
$525.00	2%	$5.25	$530.25	$5.30	$535.55
947.34	3	14.21	961.55	14.42	975.97
1,283.87	4.5	28.89	1,312.76	29.54	1,342.30
1,736.90	4	34.74	1,771.64	35.43	1,807.07
2,437.04	3.5	42.65	2,479.69	43.39	2,523.08
3,421.67	6	102.65	3,524.32	105.73	3,630.05
4,397.59	4.5	98.95	4,496.54	101.17	4,597.71
4,843.22	2.5	60.54	4,903.76	61.30	4,965.06
5,371.72	5	134.29	5,506.01	137.65	5,643.66
8,932.98	5.5	245.66	9,178.64	252.41	9,431.05

Part 3: Demonstrate Your Knowledge

Application Documents

Marketing yourself for a job is similar to marketing a product. In a job search, you are selecting your target market, determining the market needs, and advertising your skills that meet those needs. Finally, you must use persuasive selling techniques, such as a powerful résumé and any other application documents, to win the job.

Section A

When writing a résumé, letter of inquiry, and cover message remember this: it is the information on the first page that gets read. One-page documents are the best. Imagine an employer will only have 30 seconds to look at your résumé. For each of the following headings, list the items that you most want an employer to know.

1. Experience: Student answers will vary.

2. Education: Student answers will vary.

3. Activities: Student answers will vary.

4. Awards and Honors: Student answers will vary.

Section B

Do not let the objective section (or any section of the résumé) slam the door in your face. Take the time to customize your résumé and other application documents for the specific job for which you are applying. If you write and store your résumé electronically, it is easy to customize.

Read the following scenario and answer the questions using complete sentences.

Stihl is a British company that sells power tools. It has an opening for a marketing assistant. The applicant must be bilingual in German and English. Greta is excited about the opening and writes an objective that includes "to use my fluency in German."

1. Should Greta keep this objective when she applies for other jobs?

   Student answers will vary.

2. If she does include this objective, how might it hurt her chances for jobs that do not require German?

   Student answers will vary.

Chapter 30   Preparing for Your Career   **261**

Name _____

3. If a job does *not* require German, should she leave out the fact that she is fluent in the language? Give your reason.
   Student answers will vary.

Section C

You should always speak with your references before listing them. Make sure you have their permissions to be used as references. Also, ask whether they can honestly give you a good reference. Finally, tell them about the types of jobs you are looking for and the skills you want to emphasize. Read each of the following situations. Then, answer the questions using complete sentences.

Amelie, an A student, asked her English teacher to be a reference. However, when she asked him, he said, "You should find someone who would have better things to say about you." After further questioning, Amelie learned that the teacher had confused her with someone else.

1. What might have happened if the teacher had not made that comment, and Amelie had not asked him to be a reference?
   Student answers will vary.

Manuel was applying to art school. He used one of his high school art teachers as a reference. After he submitted the application, he showed the teacher a portrait that had won first prize at a local art show. The teacher said, "You never could draw hands well."

2. How might this reference harm Manuel's chances of getting into art school? What could Manuel have done?
   Student answers will vary.

Johnny was proud of a distant relative who was the president of a large corporation. When Johnny asked the man to be a reference, he agreed. What Johnny did *not* know was that the man deeply resented being used by people he hardly knew.

3. How could Johnny have found this out? Who might have been a better reference for him?
   Student answers will vary.

Copyright Goodheart-Willcox Co., Inc.

Part 4: Be Your Own Leader

Leaders Keep Track: Building a Leadership Portfolio, Part 2

"A picture is worth a thousand words." A leadership portfolio is like a picture for you. For some people, it might be easy to sit in an interview or talk with someone about what you have done. However, when you have the documents or examples to prove it, people listen.

To build your *picture portfolio*, you will need to identify 10 instances when you successfully demonstrated your leadership skills. You will create one page for each time, totaling 10 separate pages. You can keep your portfolio digitally or in a hard-copy format. If using paper, make sure to print your pages in color. Each page will contain a title, the documentation or example, and a one- or two-sentence summary describing your leadership skills.

Title: Use a headline in 24 pt. size or higher font. Use the same font for each page. Make the font easy to read. A title should be no more than three or four words. For example, State CTSO Leadership Conference.

Example: The example can be a picture, a certificate, a letter, a program, a schedule, or some other proof of your participation. Scan your proof and insert into the document.

Summary: Write a one- or two-sentence summary. For example, "In November 2012, FOCUS training taught us how to develop a vision at the state leadership conference."

Page Layout: Be creative. Lay it out anyway you want. Just make sure the focus is on the information and the layout is clean, professional looking, and is not visually distracting.

Make a list of the ten pages that you will include in the portfolio and the proof you will use for each.

Page 1 Title: Student answers will vary.

Example: _____

Summary: _____

_____

Page 2 Title: Student answers will vary.

Example: _____

Summary: _____

_____

Page 3 Title: Student answers will vary.

Example: _____

Summary: _____

_____

Chapter 30   Preparing for Your Career   **263**

Name _____

Page 4 Title: <u>Student answers will vary.</u>

Example: _____

Summary: _____

_____

Page 5 Title: <u>Student answers will vary.</u>

Example: _____

Summary: _____

_____

Page 6 Title: <u>Student answers will vary.</u>

Example: _____

Summary: _____

_____

Page 7 Title: <u>Student answers will vary.</u>

Example: _____

Summary: _____

_____

Page 8 Title: <u>Student answers will vary.</u>

Example: _____

Summary: _____

_____

Page 9 Title: <u>Student answers will vary.</u>

Example: _____

Summary: _____

_____

Copyright Goodheart-Willcox Co., Inc.

Page 10 Title: *Student answers will vary.*

Example: _____

Summary: _____

_____

_____

Name _____ Date _____ Period _____

CHAPTER 31 Entrepreneurship

Part 1: Check Your Knowledge

Matching

Write the correct term for each definition on the line provided.

Key Terms

business operations
business plan
corporate formality
DBA license
entrepreneur
entrepreneurial discovery process
entrepreneurship
feasible
franchise
franchise agreement
franchise fee
franchisee
franchisor
general partnership
limited liability
limited partnership (LP)
partner
partnership agreement
self-assessment
sole proprietor
stock
stockholder
unlimited liability

1. The person who buys the right to sell the brand products of a company.
   franchisee

2. Means that something can be done successfully.
   feasible

3. A record or procedure that corporations are required by law to complete.
   corporate formality

4. The form of ownership in which two or more people own the business.
   partnership

5. License needed to register a business.
   DBA license

Copyright Goodheart-Willcox Co., Inc. 265

6. A tool that helps a person understand personal preferences and identify strengths and weaknesses.
   self-assessment

7. Taking on both the risks and responsibilities of starting a new business.
   entrepreneurship

8. A written document that describes a new business, how it will operate, and make a profit.
   business plan

9. The legal document that sets up a franchise.
   franchise agreement

10. The day-to-day activities necessary to keep a business up and running.
    business operations

11. A person who buys shares of stock in a corporation and is an owner.
    stockholder

12. A form of partnership where there is one managing partner and at least one limited partner.
    limited partnership (LP)

13. A person who starts a new business.
    entrepreneur

14. The company or person who owns the business and the brand.
    franchisor

15. The one person who owns a business and is personally responsible for all of its debts.
    sole proprietor

16. The right to do business using the brand and products of another business.
    franchise

17. An owner's legal responsibility for all of the debts and actions of the business.
    unlimited liability

18. Form of business in which all partners have unlimited liability.
    general partnership

19. Finding a need for a product or service.
    entrepreneurial discovery process

20. Legal document detailing how much each partner will invest, each partner's responsibilities, and how profits are to be shared.
    partnership agreement

Chapter 31   Entrepreneurship

Name _____

True or False

Decide whether each statement is true or false and enter *T* or *F* on the line provided. If the statement is false, rewrite the statement to make it true.

1. Many marketing professionals become entrepreneurs.   True

2. Entrepreneurs do *not* need excellent communication skills.   False. Entrepreneurs need excellent communication skills.

3. The higher the risk, the greater potential for both reward and loss.   True

4. Limited liability means a partner or owner can lose more than the amount originally invested by that person. They are personally liable for the debts of the business.
   False. Limited liability means that a partner or owner cannot lose more than the amount originally invested by that person. They are not personally liable for the debts of the business.

5. A corporation is considered to be a legal entity and is viewed, in the eyes of the law, as a person.   True

6. Stock is a percentage of ownership in a sole proprietorship.   False. Stock is a percentage of ownership in a corporation.

7. LLCs are less expensive to form than sole proprietorships and partnerships.
   False. LLCs are more expensive to form than sole proprietorships and partnerships.

8. Business failure rates are low for new businesses.   False. Business failure rates are highest for new businesses.

9. A franchise fee is the money that a franchisor pays the franchisee for the right to use the business brand name and sell its products.   False. The franchise fee is the money that a franchisee pays the franchisor for the right to use the business brand name and sell its products.

10. The initial cost to buy the franchise can be large.   True

Part 2: Marketing by the Numbers

Installment Loan Payments

Many small businesses offer their customers installment loans as a way to pay for high-priced merchandise. An installment loan payment plan is similar to getting a loan. However, instead of getting money from a bank and repaying the bank, you repay the seller of the products, such as the retail store.

There are tables for calculating installment payments. The table is based on the interest rate and the term of the installment plan. The table then indicates how much you are charged for each dollar borrowed at a certain interest rate and term. You can then calculate the loan payment by multiplying by the number of dollars being borrowed. The following table shows an example.

Installment Payments per Dollar Borrowed				
Interest Rate (%)	12-Month Term ($)	18-Month Term ($)	24-Month Term ($)	30-Month Term ($)
8	0.08699	0.05914	0.04523	0.03689
9	0.08745	0.05960	0.04568	0.03735
10	0.08792	0.06006	0.04614	0.03781
11	0.08838	0.06052	0.04611	0.03828
12	0.08885	0.06098	0.04707	0.03875

To calculate an installment payment, find the interest rate and term in the table. Then, multiply the cost of the product by the installment payment per dollar. For example, suppose a customer is buying a $1,000 table with an installment plan at 11% interest for 18 months:

$1,000 × 0.06052 = $60.52 (monthly payment for 18 months)

In this example, the total payment for the installment plan would be $1,089.36.

$60.52 × 18 months = $1,089.36

The cost of buying a $1,000 table using that installment loan plan would be the total payment minus the cost of the product, which for this example is $89.36.

$1,089.36 – $1,000 = $89.36

Use this information to help you complete the chart on the next page.

Chapter 31   Entrepreneurship

Name _____

Fill in the following chart by calculating installment payments for a $1,000 purchase. The first one has been completed for you as an example.

Interest Rate (%)	Number of Months	Payment per Dollar	Monthly Payment	Total Payment	Cost of Installment Plan
8	12	$0.08699	$86.99	$1,043.88	$43.88
8	18	0.05914	59.14	1,064.52	64.52
8	24	0.04523	45.23	1,085.52	85.52
8	30	0.03689	36.89	1,106.70	106.70
9	12	0.08745	87.45	1,049.40	49.40
9	18	0.05960	59.60	1,072.80	72.80
9	24	0.04568	45.68	1,096.32	96.35
9	30	0.03735	37.35	1,120.50	120.50
10	12	0.08792	87.92	1,055.04	55.04
10	18	0.06006	60.06	1,081.08	81.08
10	24	0.04614	46.14	1,107.36	107.36
10	30	0.03781	37.81	1,134.30	134.30
11	12	0.08838	88.38	1,060.56	60.56
11	18	0.06052	60.52	1,089.36	89.36
11	24	0.04611	46.11	1,106.64	106.64
11	30	0.03828	38.28	1,148.40	148.40
12	12	0.08885	88.85	1,066.20	66.20
12	18	0.06098	60.98	1,097.64	97.64
12	24	0.04707	47.07	1,129.68	129.68
12	30	0.03875	38.75	1,162.50	162.50

Copyright Goodheart-Willcox Co., Inc.

Part 3: Demonstrate Your Knowledge

Entrepreneurs

The following are descriptions of three people. For each person, list the entrepreneurial traits that he or she exhibits. Refer to Figure 31-2 in the text book. Then, answer the questions that follow.

Junius is a bright young man with terrific personal drive. He has been at the head of his class since middle school and now has his choice of several college scholarships. Junius is considering a career in tax accounting or corporate law. He likes rules and predictability. If he spends a certain number hours of working, he wants to know he will earn a specific salary. He is a self-reliant person who needs little oversight, and he does not want to be responsible for anyone else.

1. Entrepreneurial traits: Student answers will vary.

Maha has a creative flair. She is the first to wear new fashions and start trends. When she came back from a family trip to Brazil, she began giving after-school dance classes at $10 an hour to teach the new dances she learned there. In addition, her hand-painted, silk sarongs were such a hit that she had to hire three helpers to keep up with the demand. Maha has so many ideas that she is always leaving one thing and going on to something new.

2. Entrepreneurial traits: Student answers will vary.

Dale is a serious student with a gift for seeing the big picture. Some people call him a wet blanket because he is often the one to point out any problems with a new idea or plan. However, when asked to come up with a better idea or plan, he always has a good one. For the past three years, Dale has led a team of science students to the state finals.

3. Entrepreneurial traits: Student answers will vary.

Answer the following question using complete sentences.

4. Assume that each of these people really wants to be an entrepreneur. Suppose that they came to you for advice. What would you say to each of them and why?

   Student answers will vary.

Chapter 31   Entrepreneurship

Name _____

Part 4: Be Your Own Leader

Leaders Keep Track: Building a Leadership Portfolio, Part 3

The last pages of your *Leadership Portfolio,* there will be a one-or two-page, double-spaced essay about yourself and a letter of recommendation from a person who knows about your capabilities as a leader. Summarize your experiences, your beliefs about leadership, your core values, and any other important information. Ask others for quotes about you that you might use in your personal essay. Tell your story creatively. Provide specific examples to help the reader know you better, even if they have never met you. You may want to review some examples of well-written college or personal essays before completing your own. Use the space that follows to draft the main points for your essay. Then, key a draft of the essay. Have a peer review the draft, then finalize the essay.

1. Draft the main points for your essay here.
   Student answers will vary.
   _____
   _____
   _____
   _____
   _____
   _____

2. Ask an adult who knows you well (*not* a relative) for a letter of recommendation. Give the person a copy of your Leadership Vitae so he or she can write a letter about your leadership skills. Give the person a deadline for returning the letter of recommendation. Add the letter to your portfolio.

Name _____ Date _____ Period _____

CHAPTER 32 Risk Management

Part 1: Check Your Knowledge

Matching

Write the correct term for each definition on the line provided.

Key Terms

burglary
controllable risk
economic risk
embezzlement
emergency
emergency action plan
fraud
hazard
human risk
insurance
insurance premium
lawsuit
market risk
natural risk
planned obsolescence
product obsolescence
risk
risk assessment
robbery
security
shoplifter
surveillance
uncontrollable risk
uninsurable risk

1. A situation that could result in injury or damage.
   hazard

2. The process of analyzing a business for possible risks.
   risk assessment

3. The process of bringing a complaint to a court for resolution.
   lawsuit

4. Occurs when a person breaks into a business to steal merchandise, money, valuable equipment or take confidential information.
   burglary

5. A negative situation caused by human actions.
   human risk

Copyright Goodheart-Willcox Co., Inc.   273

6. Evaluating and updating current products or adding new ones to replace older ones.
   planned obsolescence

7. A financial service used to protect individuals and businesses against financial loss.
   insurance

8. The potential that the target market for new products or services is much less than originally thought.
   market risk

9. A person, posing as a customer, who takes goods from the store without paying for them.
   shoplifter

10. Cheating or deceiving a business out of money or property.
    fraud

11. An unforeseen event that can cause harm to people and property.
    emergency

12. Consists of actions taken to prevent crime and protect the safety of people and property.
    security

13. A theft involving another person, often by using force or with the threat of violence.
    robbery

14. A situation that cannot be predicted or covered by purchasing insurance.
    uncontrollable risk

15. Means that an employee is stealing either money or goods entrusted to him or her.
    embezzlement

16. A detailed plan that describes what to do in case of an emergency.
    emergency action plan

17. The possibility of loss, damage, or injury.
    risk

18. Over time, the product becomes out-of-date.
    product obsolescence

19. A situation that occurs when the economy suffers due to negative business conditions in the United States or the world.
    economic risk

20. The process of observing everything going on at the business to detect and prevent crimes.
    surveillance

Chapter 32 Risk Management   **275**

Name _____

True or False

Decide whether each statement is true or false and enter *T* or *F* on the line provided. If the statement is false, rewrite the statement to make it true.

1. A controllable risk is one that can be avoided. False. A controllable risk is one that cannot be avoided, but can be minimized by purchasing insurance or implementing a risk management plan.

2. A speculative risk is the threat of loss with no chance for profit. False. A pure risk is the threat of loss with no chance for profit.

3. Natural risk is a situation caused by an act of nature. True

4. Just because your product is currently successful does not mean it will always be successful. True

5. Security policies consist of security features in a building, such as lights, alarms, locks, and computerized security systems. False. Structural security consists of security features in a building, such as lights, alarms, locks, and computerized security systems.

6. Businesses are responsible for the health and safety of customers while they are on company property. True

7. An insurance premium is the amount that is received from insurance. False. An insurance premium is the amount that is paid for insurance.

8. Property insurance usually covers losses due to fires, tornadoes, hail, accidents, burglary, and arson. True

9. An uninsurable risk is one that an insurance company will not cover. True

10. A treasury bond is a document signed by a contractor to fulfill a service agreed upon by the parties. False. A surety bond is a document signed by a contractor to fulfill a service agreed upon by the parties.

Copyright Goodheart-Willcox Co., Inc.

Part 2: Marketing by the Numbers

Insurance

Insurance is the financial service used to protect individuals and businesses against financial loss. The cost of an insurance policy is called a *premium*. Premiums are calculated on a yearly basis.

Most insurance companies allow customers to pay premiums in monthly, quarterly, or semiannual installments. They usually charge a fee for this service. For example, suppose your premium is $1,800. If you cannot pay $1,800 at once, you can divide your payments into installments. The company will charge you a service fee of $8 for each additional payment in the following way:

- If paying the entire amount at once, the bill is $1,800.
- If paying semiannually, each payment is $900 plus $8 ($908), for a total of $1,816.
- If paying quarterly, each payment is $450 plus $8 ($458), for a total of $1,832.
- If paying monthly, each payment is $150 plus $8 ($158), for a total of $1,896.

Complete the following table by calculating the payments based on the premium and fee for each column.

Insurance Premiums and Fees				
Premium/Fee	$2,452/$4.50	$5,856/$7.50	$6,252/$6.75	$9,612/$9.00
One Annual Payment				
Total for Year	2,452.00	5,856.00	6,252.00	9,612.00
Two Semiannual Payments				
Cost per Payment	1,230.50	2,935.50	3,132.75	4,815.00
Total for Year	2,461.00	5,871.00	6,265.50	9,630.00
Four Quarterly Payments				
Cost per Payment	617.50	1,471.50	1,569.75	2,412.00
Total for Year	2,470.00	5,886.00	6,279.00	9,648.00
Twelve Monthly Payments				
Cost per Payment	208.83	495.50	527.75	810.00
Total for Year	2,505.96	5,946.00	6,333.00	9,720.00
Difference between one annual payment and 12 monthly payments	53.96	90.00	81.00	108.00

1. How much more expensive is it to pay once versus 12 monthly payments?
   Between $53.96 and $108.00, depending on the premium amount

2. Why might someone want to make 12 monthly payments rather than 1 payment?
   Student answers will vary.

Chapter 32   Risk Management

Name _____

Part 3: Demonstrate Your Knowledge

Store Security

Think of a store you often visit. What types of security measures are in place? Complete the following chart by describing the listed security measures in complete sentences. If a particular security measure does not exist at the store you selected, indicate it in the space provided. When you have completed the chart, answer the questions.

Security Measures	Brief Description:
Guards	Student answers will vary.
Signs	Student answers will vary.
Video surveillance	Student answers will vary.
Locks	Student answers will vary.
Lights	Student answers will vary.
Gates	Student answers will vary.
Metal bars	Student answers will vary.
Tags on merchandise	Student answers will vary.
Payment procedures	Student answers will vary.
Other	Student answers will vary.

1. What is the name of the store? What type of merchandise does it carry? Where is it located?
   Student answers will vary.

2. How do the security measures affect the store atmosphere?
   Student answers will vary.

3. Is security a problem at this store? Explain.
   Student answers will vary.

4. How would you change security at this store?
   Student answers will vary.

Copyright Goodheart-Willcox Co., Inc.

Security Methods

Which Is Worse: The Problem or the Solution? A True Story

The women's clothing department of a large store was losing thousands of dollars to shoplifting. Since the entrance to the shopping mall was in this department, it was easy for shoplifters to slip out with stolen merchandise. To reduce the shoplifting problem, the store invested in security hangers. Each garment was placed on a hanger with a chain passed through it. The chains were locked onto the hangers, and the hangers were locked onto the racks.

To look at or try on any clothing, a customer would first have to find a salesperson. The customer would have to show the salesperson where each garment was, and the salesperson would have to unlock the hanger and garment. Only three garments could be unlocked at a time. If the customer wanted to try on more clothing, the procedure had to be started all over again. In addition, the store had *lean staffing*, meaning few employees, so salespeople were not always free to help customers when they needed it.

1. If you were looking for women's clothing, would you shop here? Why or why not?
   Student answers will vary.

2. Do you think this security method decreased shoplifting in the women's clothing department? Explain your answer.
   Student answers will vary.

3. What effect do you think the security method had on the sales in the women's department? Explain your answer.
   Student answers will vary.

4. If you were a marketing consultant, what could you suggest to improve sales?
   Student answers will vary.

5. If you were a security consultant, what other ways could you suggest to improve security?
   Student answers will vary.

Chapter 32   Risk Management 279

Name _____

Part 4: Be Your Own Leader

Effective Leaders Plan for Their Futures

Some say good leaders are born. Others say being an effective leader takes work. Maybe both views are correct. Some leaders do have the innate ability to lead, while others work to develop their skills. All leaders, however, do have a clear vision for their futures.

Great leaders not only think about the future, they turn their visions into reality. You have completed many activities in this workbook designed to help you think about where you are as a leader and how to build your leadership skills. Take time now to reflect on your leadership style and plan to increase your leadership skills. Create a plan, using the questions below to guide you.

1. Write your vision of where you see yourself in five years as a leader.
   Student answers will vary.

2. Write three SMART leadership goals for yourself. One of the goals should be short term and two of the goals should be long term, or will take more than one year to complete. Remember: S = specific, M = measurable, A = attainable, R = realistic, and T = timely.

   Goal 1
   Student answers will vary.

   Goal 2
   Student answers will vary.

   Goal 3
   Student answers will vary.

Copyright Goodheart-Willcox Co., Inc.

3. Create your plan for attaining your goals.
   Student answers will vary.
   _____
   _____
   _____
   _____

4. Ask another student, teacher, parent, or mentor to review your goals and your plan. Ask the person to write at least one additional recommendation for you to help you become a better leader.

   Name of person (print): Student answers will vary.

   Title Position: _____

   Recommendation for becoming a better leader: _____
   _____
   _____
   _____

Name _____ Date _____ Period _____

CHAPTER 33: Business Funding

Part 1: Check Your Knowledge

Matching

Write the correct term for each definition on the line provided.

Key Terms

accounts payable
accounts receivable
angel investor
asset
bootstrapping
collateral
cosigner
debt financing
equity
equity financing
fixed asset
fixed expense
liabilities
line of credit
liquid asset
operating expense
owner's equity
peer-to-peer lending
pro forma balance sheet
pro forma cash flow statement
pro forma financial statement
pro forma income statement
start-up capital
start-up costs
trade credit
variable expense
venture capitalist

1. An item of value owned by a business that may take time to sell.
   fixed asset

2. Financial statement that projects the financial progress of the business.
   pro forma income statement

3. An ongoing expense that helps to keep a business functioning.
   operating expense

4. A specific dollar amount that a business can draw against as needed.
   line of credit

Copyright Goodheart-Willcox Co., Inc.

281

5. Professional investor or investing group looking to fund new start-ups or expansions of existing companies.
   venture capitalist

6. The amount of ownership a person has in a business.
   equity

7. The initial expenses necessary to open the doors of a business.
   start-up costs

8. Financial statement based on the best estimate of future revenue and expenses for a new business.
   pro forma financial statement

9. Money owed to a business by customers for goods or services delivered.
   accounts receivable

10. The difference between a business' assets and its liabilities.
    owner's equity

11. Cash or other item a business owns that can be easily turned into cash.
    liquid asset

12. Financial statement that reports the anticipated flow of cash into and out of the business.
    pro forma cash flow statement

13. Borrowing money from investors via a website, usually for loans under $25,000.
    peer-to-peer lending

14. Private investor who wants to fund a promising start-up businesses.
    angel investor

15. The cash used to start the business.
    start-up capital

16. Expense that remains the same every month.
    fixed expense

17. Cutting all unnecessary expenses and operating on as little cash as possible.
    bootstrapping

18. An asset pledged that will be claimed by the lender if the loan is not repaid.
    collateral

19. Financial statement that reports the assets, liabilities, and owner's equity for a proposed business.
    pro forma balance sheet

20. A business' debts or what it owes to others.
    liabilities

Chapter 33 Business Funding

Name _____

21. The money a business owes to its suppliers for goods or services received.
accounts payable

22. The property or items of value owned by a business.
assets

23. Borrowing money for business purposes.
debt financing

24. A person who signs a loan with the applicant and takes on equal responsibility for repaying it.
cosigner

25. Raising money for a business in exchange for a percentage of the ownership.
equity financing

True or False

Decide whether each statement is true or false and enter T or F on the line provided. If the statement is false, rewrite the statement to make it true.

1. Most people have enough cash on hand to completely fund a business. **False. Very few people have enough cash on hand to completely fund a business.**

2. An angel investor often has business experience that will help the new company. **True**

3. Working capital is the money invested in businesses by venture capitalists. **False. Venture capital is the money invested in businesses by venture capitalists.**

4. Loans that require collateral are known as unsecured loans. **False. Loans that require collateral are known as secured loans.**

5. An overdraft agreement allows a business to write checks for more than what is in the checking account. **True**

6. Trade credit is when one business grants a line of credit to a consumer for the purchase of goods and services. **False. Trade credit is when one business grants a line of credit to another business for the purchase of goods and services.**

7. Variable expenses are expenses that do not change on a monthly basis. **False. Variable expenses are expenses that can change on a monthly basis.**

8. Marginal benefit measures the potential gains of producing more products that sell because the profit margin is higher. **True**

9. All business loan programs require a sound business plan submitted with the loan application. **True**

10. Owner's equity is also known as the owner's net worth. **True**

Part 2: Marketing by the Numbers

Pro Forma Income Statement

Each component of the business loan application process is important. One of the major parts is the pro forma financial statement that support the business plan. *Pro forma financial statements* are financial statements based on the best estimate of future revenue and expenses for a new business. A pro forma income statement projects the expected financial progress of the business. The two main sections of a pro forma income statement are *projected revenue* and *expenses*.

The following information is the projected income and expenses for each of the first three years of a new company called Electronic Horizon, LLC. Use this information to complete a pro forma income statement for this startup company.

	Y1	Y2	Y3
Sales	$119,300	$126,200	$131,500
Advertising Expenses	17,000	18,000	19,000
Rent Expenses	30,000	30,000	30,000
Insurance Expenses	2,400	2,400	2,400
Supplies Expenses	600	700	1,000
Utilities Expenses	3,600	3,600	3,600

\multicolumn{4}{c}{**Electronic Horizon, LLC** **Pro Forma Income Statement** **Year Ended December, 20--**}			
	Year 1	**Year 2**	**Year 3**
Revenue			
Sales	$119,300	$126,200	$131,500
Expenses			
Advertising Expense	17,000	18,000	19,000
Rent Expense	30,000	30,000	30,000
Insurance Expense	2,400	2,400	2,400
Supplies Expense	600	700	1,000
Utilities Expense	3,600	3,600	3,600
Total Expenses	$53,600	$54,700	$56,000
Net Income	$65,700	$71,500	$75,500

Part 3: Demonstrate Your Knowledge

Starting a New Business

This true story has five underlined phrases. Each phrase is an example of one of the terms listed below. Write the number of the phrase next to the term it matches.

__5__ Debt financing

__4__ Fixed expenses

__1__ Pro forma financial statement

__3__ Start–up capital

__2__ Start-up costs

Joe O. loved to play video games. He had been doing so all of his life. As an adult, he obtained a full-time management position in a nationally known video game retail store. Although he enjoyed the work environment, he noticed that customers who purchased the video games did not have an opportunity to play them before purchase. Upon further investigation, Joe found there was a particular video-game marketing niche whose needs were not being met in his geographical area. So, he decided to start his own business targeting this particular group of consumers.

First, he sought guidance from the local Small Business Administration (SBA) to help him write a business plan. Based on his research, he drafted financial statements that were based on his best (1) estimates of future revenue and expenses for his new business. He also investigated all of the (2) expenses necessary to open the doors of his business. He then asked (3) family members to invest cash in his entrepreneurial enterprise.

Joe O's next step was to find a suitable location for his business. He found a downtown location within walking distance to the high school and two local colleges, his primary target market. He was able to sign a lease with the owner of the site for the (4) same rental fee for three years. He also (5) contacted a local bank and obtained a loan backed by the SBA.

Joe decided to call his new company Electronic Horizon. The doors to this new business venture opened in the spring of 2013.

Chapter 33 Business Funding **287**

Name _____

Part 4: Be Your Own Leader

Leaders Create Their Futures

It takes a strong leader to successfully start and own a business. Two keys to business success is obtaining the proper funding and identifying those people who can help you build the business. There are many ways to fund a business, as you have read about in this chapter. A leader will seek out the expertise of others with more knowledge and experience in a specific area. In order to find out what funding options are available in your community, you will need to do some research and conduct an interview to learn more about entrepreneurship.

Conduct research on the types of funding available in your community. You may want to check the local chamber of commerce website, the websites of local financial institutions, a local community college or four-year college, the state business development website, venture capital firms, or the SBA. In the spaces below, identify four types of potential local funding and one specific place to apply for each type.

Type of funding (i.e., commercial loan)   Location (i.e., First Federal Bank)

1. Student answers will vary.   Student answers will vary.

2. _____   _____

3. _____   _____

4. _____   _____

Interview

Interview one of the following people: a small business owner, a commercial loan officer, a representative from an entrepreneurial center at a local community college or university, a local SBA officer, or a SCORE representative. Ask the person each of these questions.

1. What three factors are critical for getting funding for a new business?
   Student answers will vary.
   _____
   _____
   _____

2. What are two or three barriers to receiving new business funding?
   Student answers will vary.
   _____
   _____
   _____

3. What are the best resources for obtaining new business funding?
   Student answers will vary.
   _____
   _____
   _____

Copyright Goodheart-Willcox Co., Inc.

4. Are some types of businesses more likely to get funding? If so, which ones and why?
   Student answers will vary.

5. Are some types of businesses less likely to receive funding? If so, which ones and why?
   Student answers will vary.

6. If I were to come to you for funding a new business, what should I bring?
   Student answers will vary.

7. What leadership qualities do you look for in an entrepreneur seeking small business funding?
   Student answers will vary.